Wealth Is a System Not a Salary

A repeatable system of thinking, ownership, leverage, and long-term strategy can replace income dependence and solve the modern struggle for lasting financial freedom.

By Laura Lee

Lauxon Publishing, LLC

Published by Lauxon Publishing, LLC

Author's Note

Writing this book has been both a personal and professional journey for me. I have spent years navigating the tension between earning and creating, between comfort and growth, between doing work that fills a wallet versus doing work that fills a life. Through trial, failure, and experimentation, I have come to understand that money alone is not the metric of success—freedom, resilience, and impact are.

My hope is that this book serves as a guide and a mirror. A guide because it outlines the principles, systems, and strategies that allow anyone to build lasting wealth. A mirror because it challenges you to examine your relationship with money, work, and time, and to decide whether your current path is creating real freedom or just the illusion of it.

Wealth is not an external acquisition; it is a system you create within your life. The tools, habits, and mindset outlined in this book are meant to help you design that system consciously. Everything here is practical, actionable, and grounded in the reality that life is complex—and yet, with simplicity and intentionality, true freedom is achievable.

Table of Contents

Prologue

We live in a world that tells us wealth is a paycheck, a job title, or a lifestyle upgrade. From a young age, we are conditioned to equate effort with security, hours with income, and comfort with success. But what if everything we've been taught about money is only a fragment of the truth? What if wealth is not a number on a paycheck but a system that compounds freedom, opportunity, and impact?

This book is about seeing beyond the linear exchange of time for money. It's about recognizing the patterns, principles, and structures that allow one person—or a small team—to create lasting, compounding value. It is an invitation to reframe thinking, to shift from employee habits to owner thinking, and to understand that true security is built through systems, not illusions.

We will explore why traditional paths keep most people stuck, how mindset shapes your financial trajectory, and the strategies that transform skills, capital, and ideas into scalable, resilient systems. Along the way, you will discover that wealth is not about luck, timing, or working harder—it's about designing processes that serve life, not constrain it.

This journey is not about abandoning work or ambition. It is about building freedom into the work you do and the choices you make. It is about constructing a system that works for you, even when you aren't working. By the end, you will see that wealth is not a destination but a living, compounding framework for your life.

PART I:
WHY THE SALARY MODEL IS BROKEN

CHAPTER .1

THE SALARY ILLUSION

Relying on a paycheck creates the false belief that income equals security.

The salary has become the modern symbol of safety, even though it was never designed to provide it. A paycheck feels predictable because it arrives on a schedule, not because it is guaranteed. Many people confuse consistency with certainty, assuming repetition means permanence. This belief quietly shapes decisions about risk, lifestyle, and ambition. Over time, the salary becomes less a tool and more a psychological anchor. What feels stable is often fragile beneath the surface.

The illusion begins early, when success is defined as finding a good job with reliable pay. Education systems reinforce this narrative by rewarding obedience and specialization over ownership and creativity. From the start, income is framed as the finish line rather than a starting point. Few are taught to question where the money comes from or how long it will last. The focus remains on earning rather than building. This narrow framing limits what people believe is possible.

A paycheck depends on forces outside the individual's control. Employers change strategies, markets shift, and technology replaces roles without warning. Loyalty does not eliminate vulnerability, even when performance is strong. The illusion persists because disruption often feels distant until it arrives. When income stops, most people realize how little security they truly had. What was called stability turns out to be dependence.

The illusion also hides opportunity cost. Time spent maintaining income is time not spent creating systems that outlast effort. The trade feels reasonable because the exchange is immediate and familiar. Yet familiarity is not the same as effectiveness. Years can pass without progress toward true independence. The illusion survives because the cost is invisible until it is irreversible.

Security is not about how often money arrives, but about how resilient its source is. A single stream, no matter how steady, is still a single point of failure. The illusion convinces people to optimize for comfort instead of resilience. Comfort delays discomfort, but it does not eliminate risk. In many cases, it amplifies it. The salary promises peace while quietly postponing preparation.

Dependence on a paycheck reshapes identity in subtle ways. People begin to describe themselves by their roles rather than their capabilities. Work becomes something done for money instead of something that creates value independently. This shift reduces flexibility and bargaining power over time. When identity is tied to employment, change feels threatening. The illusion deepens as fear replaces curiosity.

Financial stress often persists even at higher income levels. Raises increase lifestyle before they increase freedom. Expenses rise to meet income, preserving dependence while masking it with nicer surroundings. The illusion convinces people they are advancing when they are merely upgrading constraints. Wealth is postponed in exchange for appearances. The cycle repeats because it feels like progress.

Many assume that earning more will eventually solve the problem. This belief ignores the structure underneath the income. Without systems, higher pay simply increases the scale of dependence. More income often means more obligations and fewer options. The illusion survives because growth looks like movement. In reality, direction matters more than speed.

The paycheck trains people to wait. Wait for permission, wait for approval, wait for the next deposit. This waiting mindset erodes initiative over time. Opportunities that require upfront effort without immediate pay feel risky or irresponsible. The illusion frames delayed rewards as dangerous rather than strategic. As a result, long-term wealth paths are avoided.

True security is proactive, not reactive. It is built through assets, skills, and systems that function without constant supervision. The salary illusion reverses this order by prioritizing short-term certainty over long-term control. What feels safe today can create vulnerability tomorrow. The cost is rarely felt immediately. That delay is what makes the illusion so powerful.

The emotional comfort of a paycheck cannot be dismissed. It provides relief from immediate uncertainty and supports daily life. The problem is not income itself, but the belief that income alone is enough. When people stop questioning the structure behind their money, growth stalls. Comfort becomes the metric instead of progress. Over time, comfort hardens into fear of change.

Fear is the illusion's greatest ally. Fear of losing income discourages experimentation. Fear of instability discourages ownership. Fear of judgment discourages unconventional paths. The paycheck becomes a shield against these fears, even as it creates new ones. What begins as protection turns into a cage.

This illusion also distorts risk perception. Building something new is labeled risky, while depending on a single employer is labeled safe. The logic is reversed, but socially reinforced. Risk is judged by familiarity rather than probability. The illusion persists because it aligns with cultural norms. Challenging it requires independent thinking.

Many people sense something is wrong but cannot name it. They feel trapped despite doing everything they were told would work. This confusion leads to frustration rather than clarity. Without a new framework, the default response is to work harder. The illusion encourages effort when strategy is required.

Breaking the salary illusion does not mean rejecting work or income. It means redefining their role. Income should support systems, not replace them. Work should build assets, not just cover expenses. The illusion fades when money is seen as a tool rather than a lifeline. That shift changes everything.

Security must be redefined to escape the illusion. Real security comes from adaptability, optionality, and control. It grows when income is diversified and effort is decoupled from reward. Systems create leverage where salaries create dependence. This distinction is rarely taught but deeply consequential. Understanding it is the first step toward freedom.

When people stop equating income with safety, new questions emerge. How long would resources last if income stopped. What produces value without constant attention. Where does money flow even in uncertainty. These questions expose the weakness of the paycheck model. They also point toward better solutions.

The illusion is comfortable because it requires little imagination. A job description provides boundaries and expectations. Systems require design, patience, and responsibility. Many avoid that path because it feels uncertain. In truth, it is simply unfamiliar. Familiarity should not be mistaken for safety.

Every major shift in wealth creation has reduced reliance on fixed wages. Ownership, automation, and scalability redefine what stability looks like. Those who adapt gain resilience. Those who cling to the illusion feel increasing pressure. The world rewards systems, not salaries.

Reflection

I once believed that consistency was the same as safety, simply because money arrived on time. It took disruption to reveal how fragile that belief was. When I began questioning the structure behind income, my priorities shifted. I stopped asking how much I could earn and started asking what could endure. That single change reshaped my understanding of wealth.

"Security is not the absence of risk, but the presence of options."
— Unknown

Chapter .2

Why Hard Work Alone Keeps People Stuck

Effort without systems often leads to exhaustion instead of wealth.

Hard work has long been praised as the universal solution to financial struggle. From an early age, people are taught that effort guarantees progress. The harder you work, the story goes, the further you will go. This belief feels fair, moral, and motivating. Yet for many, years of hard work lead to fatigue rather than freedom. The disconnect between effort and outcome is rarely questioned.

Effort is visible, measurable, and socially rewarded. Long hours signal responsibility and discipline. Sacrifice becomes a badge of honor rather than a warning sign. When progress stalls, the default response is to work even harder. This creates a cycle where effort increases but results remain flat. Exhaustion replaces curiosity, and burnout replaces strategy.

Hard work without direction is like pushing a car with the parking brake engaged. Energy is expended, but momentum never builds. Without leverage, effort resets to zero each day. Nothing compounds, nothing accumulates, and nothing continues without you. The worker must always be present for value to exist. This structure guarantees limitation.

Many people mistake busyness for productivity. Full calendars and packed schedules create the illusion of forward motion. Activity feels like progress, even when it produces no lasting value. The mind is occupied enough to avoid deeper questions. Over time, motion replaces meaning. The system rewards effort while quietly ignoring outcomes.

The modern economy amplifies this problem. Productivity tools allow people to do more work, faster. Expectations rise to absorb the extra capacity. Efficiency increases output but not ownership. The worker becomes more effective at generating value for others. Hard work scales benefits upward, not outward.

Effort is not the enemy, but it is incomplete on its own. Wealth is created when effort is embedded into systems. Systems capture work once and deliver value repeatedly. Without systems, effort evaporates as soon as it stops. This is why so many hardworking people remain financially fragile. Their labor has no memory.

People often cling to hard work because it feels controllable. You can always choose to work more hours. Building systems requires uncertainty, learning, and delayed rewards. That discomfort pushes many back toward effort-based solutions. Hard work becomes a coping mechanism rather than a strategy. It feels safer even when it fails.

There is also a moral narrative attached to effort. Society praises those who grind and shames those who seek leverage. Rest is framed as laziness, and efficiency as cutting corners. This framing protects the status quo. It keeps people trading time instead of questioning structure. The system benefits from unquestioned effort.

Hard work creates diminishing returns when applied linearly. Each additional hour produces less impact than the one before it. Fatigue reduces quality, creativity, and judgment. Eventually, more work produces worse outcomes. Yet the response is rarely to step back and redesign. Instead, people push harder into the same constraint.

This dynamic creates resentment over time. Workers feel underpaid, undervalued, and unseen. They followed the rules but did not receive the promised outcome. The frustration is often internalized as personal failure. Few realize the flaw is not effort, but the model itself. Hard work was never meant to create freedom on its own.

Systems, unlike effort, are non-linear. A small amount of well-placed work can produce outsized results. Automation, delegation, and scalability allow value to persist without constant input. Systems reward thinking before doing. They require upfront effort, but reduce ongoing strain. This is why builders eventually outpace grinders.

The transition from effort to systems is uncomfortable. It requires slowing down to think, plan, and design. This pause feels risky to those conditioned to equate motion with safety. Yet without the pause, nothing changes. Momentum in the wrong direction is still wasted energy. Systems redirect effort toward permanence.

Many fear that stepping back will cause them to fall behind. In reality, it often creates clarity. When effort is examined, inefficiencies become obvious. Redundant tasks, low-impact work, and misaligned goals surface. Systems eliminate these drains. Hard work alone rarely does.

The highest-paid individuals are rarely the hardest working by raw hours. They are the ones whose decisions affect systems. Their effort is concentrated at leverage points. One choice can influence outcomes for years. This is not luck, but structure. They work differently, not necessarily more.

Hard work keeps people stuck when it becomes an identity. When self-worth is tied to effort, rest feels threatening. Change feels like betrayal of values. This attachment prevents evolution. Growth requires letting go of what once worked. Systems represent that next stage.

The goal is not to eliminate effort, but to preserve it. Systems protect effort from being wasted. They allow work to compound instead of disappear. Without systems, even the strongest work ethic eventually collapses under its own weight. Sustainability requires structure.

Understanding this distinction is liberating. It explains why struggle persists despite discipline. It reframes the problem from personal inadequacy to structural misalignment. With this insight, new options emerge. Effort can finally serve progress instead of replacing it.

Hard work is a powerful input, but a poor strategy on its own. When paired with systems, it becomes transformative. When isolated, it becomes exhausting. The difference determines whether someone advances or stalls. Wealth flows to systems, not sweat alone. This truth changes how work is approached forever.

Chapter .3

The Rising Cost of Stability

Modern living expenses are outpacing wages, making traditional paths unsustainable.

Stability used to mean predictability, affordability, and gradual progress. Today, it often means constant pressure masked as normal life. Housing, healthcare, education, and basic living costs rise faster than incomes across most professions. What once required one income now often requires two. Even then, many households feel behind. Stability has quietly become more expensive than ever before.

Wages grow incrementally, but costs move in jumps. Rent increases arrive suddenly. Insurance premiums spike without warning. Tuition climbs regardless of results. These expenses are non-negotiable for most people. When costs rise faster than pay, effort alone cannot close the gap. Stability becomes something to chase rather than something to stand on.

This shift creates a subtle form of financial anxiety. People appear stable on the surface while feeling stretched underneath. Bills are paid, but margins disappear. Savings shrink or never form. Emergencies feel catastrophic instead of manageable. Stability becomes fragile when it relies on uninterrupted income.

The traditional promise was simple. Get educated, work consistently, and gradually improve your situation. That promise assumed costs would remain proportional to earnings. That assumption no longer holds. Productivity has increased, but purchasing power has not kept pace. The math no longer works the way people expect.

Inflation is often discussed abstractly, but it is lived concretely. It shows up as smaller grocery bags, higher deductibles, and delayed goals. It forces trade-offs that didn't exist before. Vacations become rare. Retirement becomes uncertain. The cost of standing still keeps rising.

Many respond by tightening budgets rather than questioning systems. Frugality helps, but it has limits. You can only cut expenses so far before quality of life erodes. Stability should not require constant sacrifice. When it does, the structure is flawed. No amount of discipline can permanently offset structural imbalance.

The rising cost of stability changes behavior. People delay major life decisions. Marriage, children, homeownership, and entrepreneurship feel risky. These delays are rational responses to financial pressure. Yet they carry emotional and social consequences. Stability becomes something postponed rather than experienced.

Debt fills the gap between income and costs. Credit cards, loans, and financing options smooth short-term pain. Over time, they harden into obligations. What feels like stability is often borrowed time. The appearance of normalcy is maintained at the cost of future freedom. This trade-off is rarely acknowledged upfront.

Employers are not immune to these pressures. Businesses face rising costs as well. Benefits shrink, job security declines, and roles consolidate. Workers are asked to do more with less. Stability erodes on both sides of the paycheck. The system strains under its own weight.

The idea of a stable job becomes misleading. Roles change faster than people can adapt. Skills expire, departments vanish, and entire industries transform. Stability tied to position rather than adaptability becomes temporary. The cost of staying employable rises alongside living expenses. Learning becomes mandatory, not optional.

Geography intensifies the problem. Economic opportunity concentrates in expensive areas. Lower-cost regions often offer fewer options. People choose between affordability and access. Stability requires trade-offs that didn't exist in prior generations. Mobility becomes both an opportunity and a burden.

This environment rewards those who control assets rather than rely on wages. Assets adjust with inflation more effectively than salaries. Systems scale as costs rise. Those without systems absorb every increase personally. Stability becomes asymmetrical, favoring builders over earners.

Many feel this pressure but lack language for it. They blame themselves for falling behind. They work harder, save more aggressively, and still feel stuck. The problem is not individual failure. It is a shifting economic landscape. Recognizing this is empowering, not discouraging.

The rising cost of stability exposes the weakness of linear income models. When expenses compound and income does not, imbalance is inevitable. Stability requires leverage to keep pace. Without it, effort becomes defensive rather than progressive. The goal shifts from growth to survival.

This reality forces a choice. Either accept shrinking margins as normal, or redesign the approach to money entirely. Systems offer an alternative path. They grow with complexity instead of being crushed by it. Stability then becomes dynamic, not static. It adapts instead of breaking.

Understanding this shift is critical. It explains why traditional advice feels outdated. It clarifies why following the rules no longer guarantees results. Stability has changed definition. It now depends on resilience, scalability, and control. The sooner this is acknowledged, the sooner solutions become visible.

The rising cost of stability is not a temporary phase. It is a structural trend. Responding with outdated models creates frustration. Responding with systems creates options. Wealth is no longer about keeping up. It is about designing something that moves ahead.

CHAPTER .4

THE DEBT TRAP MASQUERADING AS PROGRESS

Consumer debt is designed to delay wealth while rewarding short-term comfort.

Debt is often presented as a tool for advancement rather than a liability. Financing is framed as access, convenience, and opportunity. Advertisements celebrate what debt allows people to buy, not what it costs them to keep. Monthly payments soften the psychological impact of large purchases. Progress feels affordable when it is divided into small obligations. The trap works because it feels reasonable.

Consumer debt thrives on normalization. Carrying balances is treated as standard behavior rather than a warning sign. Credit cards, auto loans, and personal financing are woven into everyday life. Few question why so many people need borrowed money to maintain normal lifestyles. The system rewards spending before saving. Debt becomes the bridge between desire and delay.

The danger of consumer debt lies in its compounding effect. Interest quietly extracts future income to pay for past choices. Each dollar borrowed reduces the flexibility of tomorrow's decisions. While income feels earned, interest feels invisible. Over time, the gap widens between what is made and what is kept. Progress slows even as effort remains constant.

Debt changes how people think. Decisions become reactive instead of strategic. Short-term relief replaces long-term planning.

Opportunities are evaluated based on immediate affordability rather than long-term return. The future becomes something to manage rather than build. Debt narrows perspective while pretending to expand options.

Many forms of consumer debt are justified as necessities. Reliable transportation, education, and housing are real needs. The issue is not borrowing itself, but the structure surrounding it. Loans are often extended beyond what creates lasting value. The line between investment and consumption blurs. Debt meant to help ends up hindering.

Lifestyle debt is particularly deceptive. It finances comfort without increasing capability. Newer cars, upgraded homes, and discretionary spending feel like progress. Yet none of these generate income or reduce future dependence. They increase fixed costs and reduce margin. The appearance of success replaces the substance of it.

Minimum payments reinforce the illusion. They suggest manageability while extending repayment indefinitely. Paying the minimum preserves comfort but maximizes interest. Progress feels steady while wealth quietly drains. The system is optimized for duration, not resolution. Freedom is postponed one payment at a time.

Debt also amplifies vulnerability during disruption. Job loss, illness, or market shifts become crises rather than setbacks. Obligations remain even when income falters. What once felt manageable becomes overwhelming. Debt removes optionality when it is needed most. Stability collapses under fixed commitments.

Social pressure accelerates the trap. People borrow to match lifestyles around them. Comparison fuels consumption, and consumption fuels debt. Few openly discuss financial strain, so the cycle continues unchecked. Debt becomes a shared silence rather than a shared problem. Normalization protects the system from scrutiny.

Consumer debt thrives because it aligns with human psychology. Immediate rewards outweigh distant consequences. Convenience beats patience. The system is not neutral. It is designed to extract value from impatience. Understanding this removes the shame and restores agency.

Escaping the debt trap requires reframing progress. Progress is not what you can afford monthly, but what you can sustain permanently. True advancement increases flexibility, not obligation. Debt that does not increase earning power delays wealth. It converts future freedom into present comfort.

This chapter is not an argument for deprivation. It is an argument for intention. Debt should serve systems, not lifestyles. When borrowing supports assets that grow or skills that scale, it can be strategic. When it supports consumption, it is corrosive. The difference determines the trajectory of wealth.

Recognizing debt as delayed cost rather than easy access changes behavior. Purchases are evaluated differently. Waiting becomes a strategy rather than a sacrifice. Freedom regains value over convenience. Progress is no longer defined by what is owned, but by what is owed.

The debt trap persists because it feels like forward motion. In reality, it is circular. Money leaves, returns smaller, and leaves again. Breaking the cycle requires stepping outside it. Wealth begins when money is allowed to stay, grow, and work. Until then, progress remains an illusion.

CHAPTER .5

THE TIME-FOR-MONEY CEILING

Trading hours for dollars places a permanent cap on earning potential.

The most common way people earn money is by exchanging time for pay. This arrangement feels logical because time is tangible and effort is visible. You show up, do the work, and receive compensation. The clarity of the exchange makes it easy to understand and accept. Yet hidden inside this model is a hard limit. No matter how skilled or dedicated someone becomes, time remains finite.

The time-for-money model creates a ceiling that effort cannot break. There are only so many hours in a day and only so much energy in a body. Overtime may increase income temporarily, but it accelerates fatigue. Promotions often increase responsibility more than freedom. Even at higher levels, income remains tied to presence. When time stops, money stops.

This ceiling is rarely acknowledged because incremental gains feel like progress. Raises, bonuses, and new titles suggest upward movement. In reality, they often represent small adjustments within the same constraint. The structure does not change, only the rate. People climb higher but remain inside the same box. The ceiling moves slightly but never disappears.

Trading time for money also limits scalability. One person can only serve so many clients, complete so many tasks, or manage so many responsibilities. Growth requires more hours or more people. Both introduce complexity and diminishing returns. Without systems, expansion becomes exhausting. The ceiling asserts itself through burnout rather than refusal.

This model also creates dependency on constant performance. Income becomes fragile because it relies on uninterrupted output. Illness, family needs, or unexpected events immediately reduce earning capacity. There is no buffer between effort and reward. Flexibility becomes a luxury rather than a feature. Time-for-money offers clarity but no resilience.

Many people attempt to break the ceiling by working multiple jobs or side hustles. While this increases income, it multiplies time demands. Life becomes fragmented into obligations. Rest becomes scarce, and focus erodes. The ceiling remains intact, only wider. Eventually, the cost exceeds the benefit.

The ceiling also affects decision-making. Opportunities are evaluated by hourly return rather than long-term impact. Tasks that do not pay immediately are deprioritized. Building assets feels inefficient compared to earning now. The model trains people to optimize short-term income at the expense of long-term leverage. This reinforces the ceiling instead of challenging it.

Technology has increased productivity but not freedom for many workers. Tools allow more output per hour, but expectations rise accordingly. Efficiency gains are absorbed by the system rather than returned as time. The ceiling adjusts to match productivity. Without ownership, tools benefit employers more than earners.

The time-for-money ceiling shapes identity as well. People begin to equate worth with productivity. Rest feels unearned, and stillness feels wasteful. Life becomes a series of transactions. This mindset limits creativity and long-term thinking. Wealth requires space to think beyond the next hour.

Breaking the ceiling requires separating income from time. This does not mean eliminating work, but changing its role. Work becomes something that builds assets rather than something that is sold repeatedly. Effort is front-loaded instead of continuously exchanged. Value persists after work stops.

Systems are the mechanism that break the ceiling. They allow one unit of effort to create many units of return. This could take the form of automation, content, ownership, or equity. The specific form matters less than the structure. Systems remember your work when time cannot.

The ceiling persists because it feels fair. You are paid for what you do. Systems feel unfair because they pay you for what you built in the past. Yet fairness does not equal effectiveness. The world rewards outcomes, not effort. Systems align with that reality.

Fear often keeps people below the ceiling. Letting go of guaranteed hourly pay feels risky. The transition period is uncomfortable and uncertain. Yet staying guarantees limitation. The ceiling is safe but confining. Growth requires stepping beyond it.

Time-for-money will always exist, but it should not be the foundation of wealth. It can fund the transition, but not complete it. Without systems, income remains capped and fragile. With systems, time is reclaimed and optionality increases. The ceiling dissolves when time is no longer the bottleneck.

Understanding this ceiling changes how work is approached. Hours are no longer the unit of progress. Leverage becomes the focus instead. Effort is directed toward permanence. Wealth begins where time dependence ends.

Author Reflection

For years, I believed that if I just became better, faster, and more disciplined, everything would eventually work out. What I did not realize was that I was improving inside a fixed container. No amount of effort could change its size. Once I saw the ceiling, I stopped trying to push through it and started building beyond it. That shift transformed how I valued both my time and my work.

"You will never get rich renting out your time." — Naval Ravikant

PART II: SEEING WEALTH AS A SYSTEM

Chapter .6

Wealth Behaves More Like Engineering Than Luck

Financial success follows predictable rules that can be learned and applied.

Wealth is often portrayed as mysterious, random, or reserved for the fortunate few. Stories of overnight success and lucky breaks dominate public attention. This framing makes wealth feel inaccessible and unpredictable. When outcomes seem random, strategy feels pointless. People either hope for luck or resign themselves to limitation. Both responses prevent deliberate action.

In reality, wealth follows patterns that repeat across time, industries, and individuals. These patterns resemble engineering more than gambling. Inputs lead to outputs in consistent ways. Certain structures reliably produce results. When those structures are missing, outcomes are equally predictable. Understanding this removes wealth from the realm of chance.

Engineering focuses on systems, constraints, and optimization. Wealth operates the same way. Capital flows toward efficiency, scalability, and durability. Systems that reduce friction attract value. Systems that depend on constant effort repel it. These principles are observable, not theoretical.

Luck plays a role in timing, but it does not create sustainability. Without structure, luck is temporary. With structure, even small advantages compound. Wealth builders design for repeatability rather than one-time wins. They assume randomness and build buffers against it. This mindset changes how decisions are made.

Many people fail financially not because they lack discipline, but because they lack design. They react instead of architect. Money is managed emotionally rather than structurally. Without a framework, decisions conflict and cancel each other out. Engineering replaces impulse with intention.

Predictable wealth systems share common traits. They separate effort from reward. They scale beyond the individual. They improve over time instead of degrading. They function even when the creator steps away. These traits are not secrets. They are simply under-taught.

The myth of luck protects poor models. If outcomes are random, models cannot be questioned. Engineering exposes flaws by showing cause and effect. When results are poor, structure is examined rather than character. This shift reduces shame and increases agency. Problems become solvable.

Wealth engineering also emphasizes constraints. Every system has limits. Engineers design around them instead of ignoring them. Time, energy, and attention are finite. Systems account for this reality. Wealth grows when constraints are respected, not denied.

This approach reframes failure. Failure becomes feedback rather than identity. If a system does not work, it is adjusted. No emotion is required. This reduces fear and encourages experimentation. Progress becomes iterative instead of dramatic.

Most people already trust engineered systems in daily life. Bridges, electricity, and technology are relied on without question. Wealth is treated differently because it feels personal. When viewed objectively, it behaves the same way. Inputs, structure, and maintenance determine output.

Once wealth is seen as engineering, learning accelerates. You stop asking who got lucky and start asking how it was built. You study structure instead of stories. This creates transferable insight. One system teaches principles that apply elsewhere.

Engineering also reveals that complexity is optional. Elegant systems often outperform complicated ones. Fewer moving parts mean fewer failures. Wealth does not require constant activity. It requires thoughtful design. Simplicity compounds.

This perspective empowers action. You do not need permission or perfect timing. You need understanding and iteration. Wealth becomes a skill, not a miracle. Skills can be practiced, refined, and improved.

Seeing wealth this way removes resentment and envy. Others are no longer competitors for luck. They are examples of applied systems. Learning replaces comparison. Curiosity replaces frustration.

Engineering thinking marks a turning point. It moves you from hoping to building. From reacting to designing. From effort to structure. Once this shift occurs, wealth stops feeling distant. It becomes a problem you know how to solve.

The rest of this book builds on this foundation. Each chapter adds components to the system. Together, they form something reliable. Wealth is no longer a mystery. It is an outcome of design.

Chapter .7

The Difference Between Income and Wealth

Income feeds your lifestyle, but systems build your future.

Income and wealth are often used interchangeably, but they are fundamentally different. Income is what flows in to support current life. Wealth is what remains to shape future choices. Confusing the two leads to false confidence and fragile plans. Many high earners are not wealthy, and many wealthy individuals do not rely on high income. The distinction determines long-term outcomes.

Income is active and dependent on participation. It requires ongoing effort, presence, or performance. When the activity stops, income stops. This makes income inherently temporary. No matter how large it becomes, it must be continuously maintained. Wealth, by contrast, is persistent.

Wealth exists independently of daily effort. It is stored in assets, systems, and ownership. These structures continue to produce value over time. Wealth creates income, but income does not automatically create wealth. This asymmetry is rarely explained. Understanding it changes financial priorities.

Many people optimize income while neglecting wealth. Raises are celebrated, but assets are postponed. Lifestyle expands to match earnings. The gap between earning and owning widens. This creates the illusion of progress while increasing vulnerability. Income feels good, but it does not protect the future.

High income can delay wealth building by masking inefficiencies. Money covers mistakes that would otherwise force change. Comfort reduces urgency. Without intentional structure, income becomes a substitute for planning. Eventually, the underlying weakness is exposed.

Wealth compounds, while income resets. Each paycheck starts from zero. Assets build on prior value. Time works for wealth and against income. The longer wealth exists, the more powerful it becomes. Income remains linear regardless of duration.

This difference affects how decisions are evaluated. Income-focused thinking asks how much something pays now. Wealth-focused thinking asks what it creates over time. The same opportunity can look attractive or irrelevant depending on perspective. Time horizon changes everything.

Wealth also creates optionality. It allows choices to be made without immediate financial pressure. Income-only living removes that freedom. Decisions become constrained by the next paycheck. Wealth expands the range of acceptable risks. This accelerates growth.

Many people delay wealth building until income feels sufficient. This delay is costly. Wealth grows slowly at first and rapidly later. Waiting postpones compounding. Starting early matters more than starting big. Income should fund wealth, not replace it.

The distinction also clarifies why some people seem calm during uncertainty. Wealth buffers shock. Income does not. When disruptions occur, wealth absorbs impact. Income-dependent individuals feel every fluctuation. Stability is structural, not emotional.

Wealth is not about excess consumption. It is about stored value and productive capacity. Owning less but owning well often outperforms owning more through debt. Wealth simplifies while income complicates. The goal shifts from more to enough.

Understanding this difference removes guilt around reducing income temporarily to build systems. Short-term income drops can support long-term wealth gains. Without this clarity, such moves feel reckless. With it, they feel strategic.

The transition from income to wealth focus requires restraint. It demands resisting lifestyle expansion. It requires redirecting surplus toward assets. This discipline is easier when the distinction is clear. Purpose replaces temptation.

Wealth thinking also changes how success is measured. Net worth, cash flow durability, and optionality matter more than salary. Progress becomes quieter but more meaningful. Comparison loses relevance. Personal trajectory takes focus.

Income is a tool, not a destination. When treated as the goal, it traps people in perpetual motion. When treated as fuel, it accelerates system building. Wealth is the outcome of that process. The difference is subtle but decisive.

Recognizing the separation between income and wealth is foundational. It sets the direction for every chapter that follows. Without this understanding, effort is misallocated. With it, strategy becomes clear. The future shifts from uncertain to designed.

CHAPTER .8

WHY RICH PEOPLE BUILD BEFORE THEY EARN

Wealth creators focus on assets first and income second.

Most people are taught to earn first and build later. The assumption is that income must come before ownership. This sequence feels safe because it prioritizes certainty. Yet those who create lasting wealth often reverse the order. They build something valuable before it pays them. This inversion explains much of the gap between earners and owners.

Building before earning requires delayed gratification. Effort is invested without immediate reward. Time, energy, and resources are committed upfront. This feels uncomfortable to those conditioned to immediate pay. Yet this discomfort is temporary. The payoff, when it arrives, is persistent.

Assets are created, not discovered. They begin as ideas, skills, or systems with no income attached. Early stages often look unproductive by traditional measures. There are no paychecks to validate progress. Builders rely on vision rather than feedback. This phase filters out those dependent on immediate reinforcement.

Rich people understand that income is a symptom, not a cause. Revenue flows from value that already exists. They focus on creating that value first. Once built, income becomes a byproduct rather than a pursuit. This reduces stress and increases leverage.

Earning first encourages consumption. Building first encourages reinvestment. When income arrives before systems, it is easily absorbed by lifestyle. When systems come first, income has a destination. Structure directs behavior. Order determines outcome.

Building also allows control over economics. Owners set terms, adjust pricing, and decide scale. Earners accept terms set by others. Control compounds over time. Small decisions made repeatedly create large differences. Ownership captures that compounding.

This approach also changes risk. Building feels risky because it lacks immediate return. Earning feels safe because it pays now. In reality, earning without assets is riskier long-term. It depends on continued permission. Building creates autonomy. Risk is front-loaded but finite.

Rich people are willing to look unproductive in the short term. They invest in foundations others overlook. While peers optimize income, they optimize structure. The difference is invisible at first. Over time, it becomes impossible to ignore. Systems outperform salaries.

Building before earning also creates optionality. Once assets exist, income can be turned on or off. This flexibility is rare among earners. It allows strategic pauses and pivots. Time becomes an ally rather than a constraint.

This mindset requires confidence in process rather than outcome. Builders trust that value will eventually be recognized. They measure progress by improvement, not pay. This internal metric sustains momentum. External validation arrives later.

Many people could build but choose not to. The initial phase feels slow and uncertain. Society rewards visible income, not invisible construction. Builders accept this trade-off. They sacrifice recognition now for freedom later.

Education often reinforces the earning-first model. Degrees are pursued for job placement rather than value creation. Skills are framed as employability rather than scalability. This shapes expectations. Breaking from it requires independent thinking.

Building does not mean quitting income entirely. Many build alongside earning. The key is priority. Time and energy are allocated toward assets before comfort. Income becomes support, not focus. This balance accelerates progress.

The results of building-first thinking appear nonlinear. Long periods of little return are followed by sudden expansion. This pattern confuses observers. It is mistaken for luck. In reality, it is delayed consequence.

Understanding this sequence changes behavior immediately. It reframes unpaid effort as investment. It legitimizes patience. It shifts focus from earning more to building better. Wealth becomes something constructed intentionally.

Rich people are not allergic to work. They are allergic to work that disappears. They choose to build before they earn because they understand permanence. Income fades. Assets remain. That distinction defines their strategy.

Chapter .9

Systems Multiply While Effort Divides

One well-designed system can outperform years of individual labor.

Effort alone is inherently limited. Every person has only so much time, energy, and focus. Working harder or longer can produce marginal gains, but it cannot escape these natural limits. Systems, on the other hand, scale beyond the individual. They capture effort once and allow it to produce value repeatedly. This is the fundamental difference between working for money and building wealth.

A system is a repeatable process that produces outcomes without requiring constant supervision. It can be a business model, an investment framework, or an automated workflow. Once designed and implemented, it continues to generate returns. Effort is multiplied through leverage, delegation, and automation. One hour spent designing a system can yield years of benefit. The payoff is exponential rather than linear.

Effort divides because it is consumed immediately. Every task requires input, and when input stops, output stops. Without a system, progress resets daily. The laborer trades hours for value, never escaping the time-for-money trap. In contrast, systems persist. The initial input continues to produce, even when the creator steps away. Work is no longer tied directly to presence.

Systems also reduce human error and inefficiency. When processes are clearly defined, they are less dependent on memory, motivation, or perfection. They create consistency and predictability. Effort is fragile; systems are robust. The strongest results emerge not from more hours but from smarter design.

Another advantage of systems is scalability. Effort scales poorly because the individual cannot multiply themselves. Systems can scale horizontally or vertically. Horizontal scaling involves replication across people or units. Vertical scaling involves deepening impact per unit. The difference is immense: effort remains linear, systems compound.

Systems also foster resilience. When disruption occurs, they can absorb shocks. Redundant processes, automated flows, and diversified assets allow continuity. Effort alone offers no such protection. A person cannot work harder when unforeseen events remove their capacity. Systems maintain function without constant input.

Many people fail to adopt systems because they undervalue design. Effort is visible and tangible, while system-building is invisible work. The upfront investment feels intangible and slow. Short-term thinking favors immediate reward over long-term leverage. Yet those who persist reap disproportionate benefit.

The principle of multiplication applies across life, not just business. Skills, habits, knowledge, and capital can all be embedded into systems. Writing a book, creating a course, or developing software allows one to share effort with thousands. Time and energy are transformed into enduring value. Effort divides; systems multiply.

Systems also change decision-making. When processes are defined, choices are guided by structure rather than impulse. This reduces fatigue and increases consistency. Progress becomes inevitable, not random. Effort alone leaves outcomes vulnerable to variation in performance, mood, or circumstance.

Even small systems outperform raw effort over time. A habit, a routine, or a simple automation frees bandwidth and multiplies output. Cumulative systems produce compounding returns. One hour of well-designed work can surpass ten hours of unfocused effort. The distinction between effort and system is foundational to long-term wealth.

Building systems also shifts mindset from reaction to creation. Instead of responding to each task, the focus moves to designing for efficiency and impact. Labor becomes strategic. Time becomes an asset rather than a constraint. Wealth grows where systems are built, not where hours are spent.

Effort without systems is like running on a treadmill. The motion is constant, visible, and exhausting. The position remains largely unchanged. Systems allow forward movement while conserving energy. Momentum continues even when input stops. The multiplier effect transforms work into wealth.

System thinking also enables delegation and collaboration. Processes can be handed to others with clarity and expectation. Effort can be shared without losing fidelity of outcome. The network effect multiplies impact exponentially. Wealth accumulates through leverage rather than sweat alone.

Ultimately, understanding the distinction between effort and systems is transformative. It changes how work is approached, time is valued, and wealth is created. Effort remains important, but its role is now strategic, not endless. The multiplier is where progress becomes exponential.

Reflection

I once believed relentless effort was the path to success. I worked long hours, thinking that endurance would be enough. When I discovered system design, everything changed. I realized that small, deliberate structures could outperform years of brute effort. That understanding reshaped my work, my time, and ultimately my wealth trajectory.

"Work smarter, not harder, and your efforts will multiply instead of divide." — Unknown

Chapter .10

The Long Game Most People Never Play

True wealth is built by optimizing decades, not months.

Many people approach money with short-term thinking. They focus on immediate income, quick wins, and instant gratification. Promotions, side hustles, and small investments dominate attention. While these actions feel productive, they rarely lead to lasting wealth. True financial success comes from strategies that unfold over years and decades, not just months. The horizon matters more than the next paycheck.

Playing the long game requires patience and discipline. Results are delayed, often invisible in the early stages. Most people become impatient and abandon strategies too soon. They measure progress using short-term benchmarks rather than cumulative growth. Wealth built slowly compounds quietly, while income-focused gains vanish quickly. Time becomes the most important variable in the equation.

The long game emphasizes compounding. Investments, knowledge, and assets grow exponentially when nurtured over time. Early contributions, even if small, multiply through persistent action. Delayed gratification enables this compounding to function effectively. Those who abandon it for immediate returns limit their future options. Small sacrifices today unlock large rewards tomorrow.

Consistency is more important than intensity. A few hours of repeated action, carefully applied over years, produces far greater results than bursts of effort. This principle applies to money, business, learning, and relationships. Effort without consistency is wasted. Systems and processes allow consistent action to continue even when motivation wanes. The long game thrives on momentum, not heroics.

The long game also changes risk perception. Decisions that seem risky in the short term may be safe over decades. Conversely, actions that seem harmless now may create long-term vulnerability. Wealth is built by evaluating decisions through a multi-year lens. Short-term thinking encourages consumption; long-term thinking prioritizes construction. Perspective is critical.

Many people fail to adopt the long game because of cultural pressures. Society celebrates immediate success stories, flashy gains, and instant recognition. Patience is rarely glorified. Building over time feels invisible compared to rapid results. This social bias makes the strategy psychologically challenging. Yet those who persevere benefit disproportionately.

Education and early career often reinforce short-term thinking. Grades, promotions, and early achievements reward speed over sustainability. Students and workers are conditioned to chase results rather than design systems. The long-term trajectory remains hidden. Learning to think in decades rather than years is a mental adjustment that few make.

Playing the long game also encourages diversification. Long horizons allow for experimentation across multiple strategies. Failures become lessons rather than catastrophes. Systems and assets have time to recover and grow. Flexibility becomes an advantage. Short-term thinking magnifies losses; long-term thinking absorbs them.

The long game is incompatible with fear of uncertainty. Many avoid decisions that do not produce immediate payoffs. Builders embrace risk strategically, knowing time will amplify rewards. Opportunity cost is viewed through decades, not months. Fear diminishes as perspective expands. Patience is a form of power.

Ultimately, the long game aligns with reality. Most wealth does not appear overnight; it grows gradually and silently. Income alone cannot replicate this effect. Effort without strategy cannot endure decades. Systems, patience, and vision create true financial freedom. Those who adopt the long game play where others cannot compete.

Chapter .11

From Employee Thinking to Owner Thinking

Ownership changes how decisions, risks, and rewards are evaluated.

Most people are trained to think like employees. Security, compliance, and following instructions dominate priorities. The focus is on completing tasks rather than creating value. Success is measured by performance reviews, promotions, and raises. While this mindset provides short-term stability, it limits long-term wealth creation. Owner thinking shifts priorities from immediate reward to strategic value creation.

Owner thinking evaluates decisions based on leverage. Each choice considers long-term consequences and potential scale. Risk is managed differently because control is prioritized over compliance. Owners focus on outcomes, not input. They ask how an action will affect assets, systems, and optionality, rather than simply how it fulfills a task. This perspective changes both behavior and results.

Risk tolerance increases with ownership. Employees often avoid risk because failure impacts immediate income. Owners understand that calculated risk can create disproportionate returns. They accept temporary discomfort for lasting advantage. This shift allows bold moves that are unavailable to those constrained by wages. Growth is a function of control and leverage, not effort alone.

Owner thinking also changes the relationship with time. Employees trade hours for pay. Owners invest time in assets that continue to generate value without direct input. The focus moves from activity to impact. Time becomes a resource to allocate strategically, rather than a currency to spend. This mindset unlocks freedom that effort alone cannot provide.

Financial decisions are evaluated differently. Owners prioritize long-term gains over short-term comfort. Spending is directed toward building rather than consuming. Investments, partnerships, and systems take precedence over instant gratification. Income is a tool to support growth, not a measure of achievement. This change in perspective is foundational to wealth creation.

Shifting to owner thinking requires reprogramming beliefs. Many fear loss, change, or uncertainty. Ownership feels riskier than employment because the outcomes are less predictable. Yet this perceived risk masks the potential upside. The ability to control outcomes outweighs the temporary discomfort of uncertainty. Mindset is the first lever of wealth.

Owner thinking also changes problem-solving. Challenges are approached as design problems rather than obstacles. Systems are built to handle complexity. Delegation, automation, and scalability become natural considerations. Solutions are long-term and adaptable, not reactive. Thinking like an owner reframes obstacles as opportunities for leverage.

This mindset also affects how value is measured. Owners assess opportunities by potential return on systems and assets, rather than immediate cash. Time, money, and effort are evaluated for their capacity to compound. Decisions are made through a lens of scalability, durability, and optionality. Value creation replaces task completion as the metric of success.

Transitioning from employee to owner thinking is gradual. It begins with small experiments in decision-making, risk-taking, and asset-building. Confidence grows as systems and outcomes prove themselves. Over time, ownership becomes the default lens. Decisions, priorities, and behaviors shift naturally. The mindset evolves from reactive to proactive.

Owners focus on leverage rather than effort. They optimize for structures that operate independently of human presence. One well-built system or relationship can outperform thousands of hours of labor. This principle distinguishes those who build wealth from those who simply earn it. Thinking like an owner aligns effort with exponential outcomes.

Ownership also fosters adaptability. In a changing economy, owners survive disruptions better than employees. They have control over resources, decision-making, and risk exposure. Flexibility becomes a strategic advantage. The ability to pivot and respond is embedded in their mindset. This security is structural, not contractual.

Ultimately, the shift to owner thinking changes identity. It replaces the safety-focused, reactive perspective of the employee with a growth-focused, proactive perspective of the owner. Decisions are guided by control, leverage, and optionality. Effort is concentrated on what scales, rather than what is consumed. Ownership becomes the lens through which all opportunities are evaluated.

Reflection

Moving from employee thinking to owner thinking was not instantaneous. Early on, I felt the tension between immediate income and long-term value creation. It took practice to prioritize systems over paychecks and leverage over hours. Today, that mindset allows me to make decisions with clarity and confidence, knowing that control and ownership compound over time.

"An employee works for a paycheck; an owner works for legacy."
— Unknown

Chapter .12

Why Comfort Is the Enemy of Growth

Wealth requires intentional discomfort in the present to gain freedom later.

Comfort is seductive because it signals safety and satisfaction. People naturally gravitate toward it, avoiding effort or risk that might disrupt ease. Yet comfort often disguises stagnation. The habits, routines, and choices that feel secure today can limit future freedom. Growth demands stepping outside familiar boundaries and enduring short-term discomfort. Without it, wealth remains aspirational rather than attainable.

Discomfort is a signal that meaningful progress is occurring. It often arises when attempting something new, taking calculated risks, or investing in the long term. The body and mind resist because evolution favors survival over expansion. Feeling uneasy is not a warning to stop; it is a sign that growth is happening. Those who embrace discomfort learn faster, adapt quicker, and build resilient systems.

Many people confuse temporary pain with permanent loss. They avoid decisions that challenge them because the short-term impact feels risky. Yet the long-term cost of staying comfortable is far greater. Income may rise, but time, flexibility, and control remain limited. Freedom is postponed while the illusion of stability persists.

Discomfort also reshapes mindset. It builds resilience, patience, and strategic thinking. Repeated exposure to manageable challenges reduces fear of failure. Individuals learn to make decisions with clarity rather than emotion. Comfort, by contrast, encourages avoidance, delay, and conformity. Progress becomes a passive hope instead of an active pursuit.

In financial terms, comfort encourages consumption over construction. People spend rather than invest, upgrade lifestyles rather than build assets, and maintain routines rather than innovate. Debt, lifestyle inflation, and dependence are reinforced. The present is pleasant, but the future is constrained. The compounding benefits of early sacrifice are lost.

Intentional discomfort is not about unnecessary suffering; it is a deliberate choice to prioritize long-term outcomes. This might mean investing time in skill-building, redirecting income into assets, or accepting uncertainty in pursuit of control. Short-term challenges are manageable, predictable, and purposeful. They are investments rather than liabilities.

Entrepreneurs and wealth builders understand this principle intuitively. Early stages of building anything—businesses, investments, systems—are uncomfortable. Results may be delayed or invisible. Emotional and financial strain is common. Yet those willing to endure discomfort gain leverage, optionality, and freedom. They trade transient ease for lasting benefit.

Discomfort also expands perspective. Facing challenges teaches lessons that comfort cannot. Adaptability, creativity, and problem-solving are developed under strain. Networks, systems, and relationships are tested and strengthened. These skills compound over time. Comfort rarely delivers such growth.

One of the greatest barriers to embracing discomfort is cultural conditioning. Society often praises immediate ease, leisure, and visible success. Pain, risk, and restraint are downplayed or stigmatized. Wealth creation requires deliberately rejecting this bias. The rewards are hidden until the future, but they are real and enduring.

The choice between comfort and growth is constant. Each decision—how to spend time, money, and energy—carries an implicit trade-off. Short-term ease sacrifices potential future freedom. Long-term focus requires intentional discomfort today. This principle separates those who create lasting wealth from those who chase temporary satisfaction.

Ultimately, comfort is not inherently bad, but unexamined comfort is dangerous. Wealth demands thoughtful risk, strategic sacrifice, and disciplined decision-making. Those who embrace discomfort gain leverage, control, and resilience. Those who chase comfort remain trapped in incremental progress.

Reflection

I used to prioritize comfort, assuming that stability equaled progress. It wasn't until I consciously chose temporary discomfort—delaying gratification, building systems, and taking calculated risks—that I saw meaningful change. That discomfort, once embraced, became the catalyst for growth and freedom, teaching me that ease today often costs liberty tomorrow.

"Discomfort is the price of admission to a meaningful life."
— Susan David

CHAPTER .13

REPLACING CONSUMPTION WITH CONSTRUCTION

Every dollar spent should be questioned for its long-term return.

Most people spend money unconsciously, prioritizing consumption over creation. Purchases are made for instant satisfaction rather than long-term impact. The latest gadgets, luxury items, or lifestyle upgrades offer temporary pleasure but no lasting value. Over time, this pattern erodes wealth and reduces financial flexibility. Construction—investing in assets, systems, and skills—produces returns that persist far beyond the initial effort. Understanding the difference transforms both financial and personal outcomes.

Consumption feels natural because it provides immediate feedback. Buying something creates instant gratification, social approval, or emotional comfort. The brain rewards short-term pleasure, reinforcing habitual spending. Yet these rewards do not compound. In contrast, construction may feel slower and less exciting at first, but it produces exponential benefits over time. The choice is between fleeting satisfaction and enduring freedom.

Replacing consumption with construction requires a shift in perspective. Every dollar should be evaluated for its future impact, not just its present enjoyment. Will it generate income, build skills, or strengthen a system? Or will it disappear with minimal return? This approach turns spending into a strategic tool rather than a passive habit. Money becomes a builder's instrument.

Construction also changes priorities and habits. It encourages saving, reinvesting, and leveraging resources. It fosters creativity in finding ways to turn assets into systems. Time is allocated toward producing value instead of merely acquiring goods. Effort and resources compound rather than vanish. This mindset gradually transforms financial behavior from reactive to proactive.

Many people resist replacing consumption because it feels like deprivation. Social norms reinforce spending and lifestyle visibility. Delaying gratification requires discipline and self-awareness. Yet the trade-off is autonomy, optionality, and long-term abundance. The discomfort of restraint is temporary; the benefits endure.

Construction-oriented spending also includes skill development. Learning, mentorship, and experience are assets that increase future earning potential. These investments improve adaptability and open doors that money alone cannot. Unlike consumer goods, skills appreciate over time. This approach multiplies returns beyond financial metrics.

Systems amplify construction. Investments, business structures, and intellectual property continue producing value with minimal ongoing input. Building before spending ensures that resources are deployed strategically. Consumption can be fun, but construction ensures independence. Assets become the engine of wealth rather than liabilities.

Replacing consumption with construction also transforms mindset. Choices become intentional rather than reactive. Impulse diminishes, and planning grows. The compounding effect is both financial and psychological. Self-discipline and strategic thinking reinforce one another. Wealth is built not by chance, but by design.

Construction can take many forms: businesses, real estate, intellectual property, or personal skills. Each dollar is a vote for the future you want to create. Every expense is an opportunity to reinforce freedom or reinforce dependence. Repetition of these decisions compounds faster than income alone ever could. Habits become systems.

Finally, the shift from consumption to construction redefines success. Pleasure is no longer the metric; progress is. Wealth is measured in control, options, and future flexibility. Spending aligns with strategic objectives. Every action either builds or diminishes freedom. Conscious construction replaces passive consumption.

Reflection

I used to spend money on what felt good in the moment, assuming that comfort equaled progress. When I began questioning each purchase and redirecting resources toward systems and assets, the trajectory of my wealth changed dramatically. The small sacrifices in the present compounded into significant freedom and optionality over time.

"Do not consume; construct, and your future will consume for you." — Unknown

Chapter .14

Learning to Think in Leverage

Progress accelerates when effort is amplified through tools, people, and systems.

Leverage is the cornerstone of exponential growth. It allows a single unit of effort to produce far greater results than raw labor alone. Without leverage, progress is linear, constrained by time, energy, and capacity. With leverage, one hour of work can ripple through systems, networks, or capital to create outcomes magnitudes larger. Understanding and applying leverage is a defining trait of wealth creators.

There are three primary forms of leverage: labor, capital, and technology. Labor leverage involves using other people's time and skills ethically to multiply output. Capital leverage uses money strategically to generate returns beyond the initial investment. Technology leverage allows a single effort to reach thousands or millions through systems, automation, or digital tools. Each form amplifies effort differently, but all share the same principle: one input can produce multiple outputs.

Leverage transforms thinking. It shifts the focus from personal productivity to structural productivity. Instead of asking, "How much can I do myself?" the question becomes, "How can I design systems that do this for me?" This reframing moves energy from execution to creation, allowing one to operate at higher levels of efficiency and impact. The mind becomes a multiplier, not just a laborer.

Without leverage, work is constrained by physical limits. Time-for-money strategies, no matter how disciplined, eventually hit ceilings. Leverage breaks these constraints. Delegating, automating, or investing creates momentum that continues even when direct effort ceases. The difference between someone stuck in linear output and someone building wealth is almost always the presence of leverage.

Learning to think in leverage requires patience and experimentation. Missteps are common because the instinct is to do tasks oneself. Trust must be developed in systems, tools, and people. Initial results may feel slower, but they compound over time. Early investment in learning and designing leverage yields outsized rewards later.

Leverage also changes risk assessment. Risks are evaluated in terms of system capacity, redundancy, and potential amplification. When mistakes occur, losses are mitigated by design rather than personal exposure. This creates a safer environment for experimentation and innovation. The fear of failure diminishes as leverage increases.

Many people underutilize leverage because of mindset constraints. Doing everything personally feels secure and satisfying in the short term. Handing off tasks or investing capital can feel uncomfortable. Yet the reward of amplified results outweighs temporary discomfort. Wealth is built by those willing to trust systems, networks, and tools.

Leverage is not static; it compounds. As systems grow and networks expand, the same input produces ever-greater outcomes. Knowledge, skills, and assets can be multiplied across time and people. Leverage magnifies both success and failure, making intentionality critical. Design matters more than effort.

The application of leverage extends beyond money. Influence, reputation, and relationships are also multiplicative. Teaching, mentoring, or creating intellectual property allows one's impact to extend far beyond personal presence. Every action has the potential to scale. Thinking in leverage transforms life from a series of tasks to a network of impact.

Ultimately, thinking in leverage changes decision-making at every level. Actions are chosen for their ability to compound rather than for immediate return. Effort is concentrated at points of maximum amplification. Systems, people, and capital work together to magnify outcomes. Linear labor becomes optional, and wealth begins to grow autonomously.

Chapter .15

Patience as a Competitive Advantage

Those who delay gratification gain access to exponential outcomes.

Patience is one of the least understood yet most powerful tools in wealth creation. Society often glorifies speed, immediate results, and instant gratification. Social media, fast consumption, and constant stimulation reinforce the desire for now. Yet true progress, particularly in building wealth, requires waiting, learning, and strategic restraint. Those who can endure temporary discomfort in pursuit of long-term rewards hold a distinct advantage.

Delayed gratification allows compounding to work its magic. Investments, businesses, and skill-building require time to grow. Small, consistent actions accumulate into exponential outcomes. Impatience truncates this process, producing incremental or fleeting results. By contrast, patience enables systems to multiply impact while reducing the friction of constant decision-making.

Patience also improves decision-making. Those who rush often overlook risk, ignore nuance, or act emotionally. Waiting allows observation, learning, and preparation. Information becomes clearer, options multiply, and outcomes improve. Strategic patience turns time into an ally rather than an enemy, giving builders the ability to respond thoughtfully instead of reactively.

In financial systems, patience often differentiates wealth builders from earners. Most people sell early for short-term gain. They trade assets, abandon plans, or spend prematurely. Those who wait capture greater rewards because value compounds over time. Understanding timing is as important as understanding opportunity.

Patience is strengthened by vision. Individuals with a clear long-term perspective are more willing to endure short-term discomfort. They see temporary sacrifice as investment in future freedom. This mindset turns waiting into action because each moment of restraint is a building block. Time itself becomes a resource rather than a constraint.

The long-term approach also allows resilience in the face of setbacks. Impatient actors often abandon plans when results are slow or challenges arise. Patient builders use adversity as data, adjusting systems while remaining committed to overarching goals. The ability to persist without panic compounds advantage over competitors who quit prematurely.

Patience is not passive; it is active restraint. It involves deliberate choice, discipline, and engagement. It requires resisting temptation, maintaining focus, and allocating resources toward long-term benefit rather than fleeting satisfaction. The disciplined wait becomes a tool, producing outcomes impossible for the impatient.

In wealth creation, patience compounds in both tangible and intangible ways. Financial assets grow. Skills appreciate. Reputation strengthens. Relationships deepen. All these elements multiply when allowed time to develop. Impatience destroys compounding by truncating growth prematurely.

Culturally, patience is undervalued. Fast results are rewarded publicly while slow wins go unnoticed. Media glorifies overnight success stories, masking years of preparation. Most people compare themselves to these illusions, reinforcing impatience. The competitive advantage is in recognizing that real wealth takes time and acting accordingly.

Ultimately, patience enables freedom. It allows builders to act with leverage, think strategically, and maintain control. It converts time into opportunity, discomfort into investment, and delay into compounding returns. Those who master patience play the long game others abandon.

Reflection

I used to seek results immediately, chasing short-term wins and visible outcomes. Over time, I realized that true advantage lies in patience—waiting, building, and letting compounding work in my favor. This shift transformed how I approach work, decisions, and wealth, turning delay into one of my greatest assets.

"Great things take time. Master patience, and you master progress." — Unknown

PART IV:
BUILDING THE CORE WEALTH SYSTEM

CHAPTER .16

DESIGNING YOUR PERSONAL WEALTH BLUEPRINT

A clear framework aligns money decisions with long-term objectives.

Wealth creation is rarely accidental. It begins with design, not hope. A personal wealth blueprint serves as a strategic map, guiding decisions about income, spending, investment, and risk. Without it, people drift from opportunity to opportunity, reacting to circumstances instead of shaping them. The blueprint ensures that each choice aligns with long-term objectives, creating cohesion and focus.

A blueprint starts with clarity on goals. What kind of lifestyle, freedom, and impact are desired? These goals provide the lens through which financial decisions are filtered. Without clarity, efforts scatter and resources are wasted. Priorities become explicit, trade-offs become manageable, and purpose directs action. Goals are the foundation upon which all systems are built.

Next, a blueprint defines financial architecture. How will income be allocated? How will savings, investments, and business ventures interact? What systems will be used to scale impact? Mapping these elements converts abstract ambition into actionable structure. Decisions are no longer reactive but guided by the framework. This reduces wasted effort and increases consistency.

A personal wealth blueprint also includes risk management. Potential pitfalls, market shifts, and personal vulnerabilities are identified and mitigated. Contingency plans are embedded in the system, allowing progress to continue even when disruptions occur. This proactive approach preserves both wealth and freedom. The blueprint transforms uncertainty into manageable scenarios.

Implementation is crucial. A blueprint is not just a document; it is a series of systems, routines, and checkpoints. Regular reviews ensure that adjustments are made as circumstances evolve. Metrics are defined to measure progress toward long-term objectives. This creates accountability and visibility. Without disciplined execution, even the best-designed blueprint fails.

Behavioral alignment is another component. The blueprint must reflect personal habits, psychology, and lifestyle. Systems are designed to support natural tendencies, not fight them. Automation, delegation, and habit formation reduce reliance on willpower. By aligning environment with objectives, progress becomes inevitable. The blueprint integrates mind, resources, and systems.

Flexibility is embedded in a strong blueprint. Life is unpredictable, and rigidity can lead to failure. A blueprint anticipates change, allowing shifts in strategy without derailing progress. Opportunities can be seized, setbacks absorbed, and systems adapted. Stability comes from structure, not from resistance to change.

Education and skill-building are also incorporated. Knowledge, experience, and networks are treated as assets within the blueprint. Investment in personal development compounds like capital. Skills are leveraged to create systems, assets, and opportunities. This creates a self-reinforcing cycle of growth.

The blueprint transforms decision-making. Each financial choice is evaluated against the framework rather than impulse or social expectation. Spending, investment, and effort are guided by strategic alignment. Short-term comfort is weighed against long-term compounding. Clarity replaces confusion.

Ultimately, designing a personal wealth blueprint is the act of taking control. It converts aspiration into plan, randomness into predictability, and effort into leverage. Wealth is no longer a hope or outcome; it is a process, structured and intentional. This framework becomes the foundation for every subsequent step in building systems, scaling impact, and creating lasting freedom.

Reflection

Before I created my own blueprint, I was reactive in every financial decision. I followed trends, took opportunities as they appeared, and measured progress by immediate gains. Once I mapped my goals, systems, and risk management, my decisions became purposeful. The blueprint turned randomness into strategy and transformed my approach to wealth forever.

"Design your financial life like you would design a bridge—it must support the weight of the future." — Unknown

Chapter .17

Cash Flow as the Fuel, Not the Goal

Income should serve system growth rather than lifestyle inflation.

Most people treat cash flow as the ultimate goal of financial life. They equate earning more with becoming wealthier. Yet income alone does not build lasting wealth. True wealth is created when cash flow is used strategically to expand systems, invest in assets, and compound over time. Treating money as fuel rather than the destination transforms the way decisions are made and progress is measured.

Cash flow is the lifeblood of any wealth system. It enables reinvestment, growth, and risk management. Without it, opportunities stall and assets cannot expand. Viewing income as a resource to feed systems creates momentum. Every dollar has purpose, contributing to the architecture of long-term financial freedom. Mismanagement of cash flow, conversely, leaves potential unrealized.

Lifestyle inflation is the primary threat to using cash flow as fuel. When each raise or bonus is consumed rather than deployed into growth, the system stagnates. Comfort is prioritized over construction. Short-term satisfaction replaces strategic planning. The danger is subtle: it feels like progress while actually slowing wealth accumulation. Income becomes a crutch rather than a catalyst.

Treating cash flow as fuel requires intentional allocation. Some money is set aside for living expenses, but the majority is directed toward assets, skills, and leverage systems. Each decision is evaluated for its potential to compound value over time. The framework ensures that money works for you, rather than you working for money. Discipline becomes the multiplier.

Cash flow also fuels optionality. Having liquidity allows for strategic moves when opportunities arise. It supports experimentation, risk-taking, and timing flexibility. The financially unprepared are forced to act reactively. Those who see cash flow as fuel act proactively, seizing advantages that others cannot. Freedom is embedded in liquidity and its strategic deployment.

The mindset shift is crucial. Most people measure success by how much they earn this month. Builders measure how much their systems and assets are growing. Money is evaluated for its capacity to accelerate long-term outcomes, not for its ability to satisfy present desires. Perspective determines use and impact.

Cash flow as fuel also aligns with system thinking. Investments, automation, and business operations all require initial input. Money becomes the energy that powers these engines. When allocated strategically, one dollar invested compounds into multiple returns over time. The initial effort multiplies indefinitely.

Leverage magnifies the impact of cash flow. When combined with labor, capital, and technology, each dollar can generate multiple streams of value. Income is transformed from a linear source into an exponential one. Systems remember and reproduce the work, amplifying results. This is the practical application of seeing money as fuel.

Behavioral discipline is essential. It requires resisting temptation, delaying gratification, and prioritizing growth over consumption. This is counterintuitive in a culture that glorifies spending. Yet each dollar invested wisely contributes to freedom, security, and optionality. The benefits accumulate silently but powerfully over time.

Ultimately, cash flow should never be confused with wealth. It is the enabler, the energy, the tool. Wealth is constructed from the systems, assets, and leverage that cash flow fuels. Income without structure is fleeting; cash flow directed toward system growth creates durability, independence, and freedom.

Reflection

I spent years chasing bigger paychecks, equating income with progress. Only when I shifted my mindset and treated cash flow as fuel for systems did I see exponential growth. Redirecting money toward assets, automation, and scalable ventures transformed both my financial trajectory and my sense of freedom. Cash flow became the engine, not the destination.

"Income is temporary; assets are permanent." — Unknown

CHAPTER .18

ASSET TYPES THAT CREATE FINANCIAL GRAVITY

Certain assets naturally attract more money, time, and opportunity.

Not all assets are created equal. Some generate recurring income, appreciate in value, or create leverage over time. These are assets with financial gravity: they pull in money, opportunities, and even other assets. Understanding which assets possess this property is critical to building lasting wealth. Without them, income may exist, but wealth does not accumulate.

Real estate is a classic example of financial gravity. Property can generate rental income, appreciate over time, and provide leverage through mortgages. A single property, properly managed, can produce returns that far exceed the effort invested. Real estate also acts as collateral, enabling further investment opportunities. Its gravitational pull attracts both income and financial flexibility.

Equities and ownership stakes are another powerful type of asset. Shares in businesses provide both dividend income and capital appreciation. Equity positions align interests with growth, creating the possibility of exponential returns. Ownership transforms participation into leverage. When structured correctly, these assets generate recurring value independent of day-to-day effort.

Intellectual property also possesses gravity. Patents, books, software, and content can continue generating income long after the initial creation. Unlike labor, these assets are not limited by time or physical presence. One creation can reach millions repeatedly, multiplying impact and revenue. Financial gravity is amplified by reach and replication.

Skills and networks, though intangible, act as gravitational assets. Rare, high-value skills attract income, opportunities, and partnerships. Strong networks provide access to knowledge, capital, and collaboration. Unlike consumable income, these assets appreciate with use. Investing in human and social capital compounds over a lifetime.

The key principle is that assets with gravity generate more than they consume. They are self-reinforcing and scalable. Each unit of effort or capital applied produces magnified returns. Financial gravity is not just about money—it is about freedom, flexibility, and influence. These assets create optionality for future decisions.

Diversification strengthens gravitational pull. Combining different types of high-leverage assets reduces risk while maintaining momentum. Real estate, equity, intellectual property, and skills complement one another. When one slows, another accelerates, maintaining system stability. This mix compounds over time, creating durable wealth.

Recognizing financial gravity changes decision-making. It prioritizes acquisitions, investments, and development toward assets that attract resources. Consumption and low-leverage income sources are deprioritized. Time and energy are focused where returns are amplified. Strategy replaces impulse.

Financial gravity also accelerates wealth beyond direct financial returns. Assets can attract partnerships, mentorship, and other forms of leverage. Social and intellectual returns compound alongside monetary ones. Systems amplify their own value, creating an ecosystem rather than isolated gains. The effect grows over decades.

Ultimately, building wealth requires prioritizing assets that possess financial gravity. They pull in income, opportunities, and leverage. They are persistent, scalable, and self-reinforcing. Focusing on these assets transforms income into durable wealth and converts effort into compounding influence. The gravitational approach ensures that your resources work for you instead of being consumed by you.

Reflection

I used to invest in what felt comfortable or familiar rather than what attracted value. Once I focused on assets with financial gravity, my wealth began to grow independently of my direct effort. Understanding which assets pull money, time, and opportunity toward you was a turning point in my financial journey.

"Some assets attract wealth like gravity; others just consume your energy." — Unknown

Chapter .19

Turning Skills into Scalable Assets

Knowledge becomes powerful when it is packaged and repeatable.

Skills are valuable, but their impact is often limited by time. One person can only apply their expertise to a finite number of tasks or clients. To escape this limitation, skills must be transformed into scalable assets—products, systems, or intellectual property that multiply impact beyond individual effort. This shift converts personal competence into compounding value.

The first step is identifying high-leverage skills. These are abilities that solve problems others are willing to pay for, teach, or replicate. Not every skill scales equally. Technical knowledge, creative capabilities, and leadership expertise often have higher potential for leverage. Choosing wisely ensures that the skill can generate repeated returns.

Packaging skills is essential. Teaching, consulting frameworks, online courses, software, or content transforms expertise into assets. One client interaction becomes one product or system available to thousands. Documentation, automation, and replication are critical. The value of skill is no longer limited to personal labor.

Repetition and distribution create scalability. A well-designed system allows one skill to impact countless users simultaneously. Digital products, intellectual property, and training programs are examples of this principle in action. Scaling does not dilute quality if systems are properly designed. Effort invested early continues to produce long after initial input.

The mindset shift is profound. Practitioners often measure their value by how much time they spend applying skills. Builders measure by how many systems, products, or assets are generated. Work becomes about design, reach, and durability. Time no longer limits value; systems amplify it.

Leverage enhances skill-based assets. Delegating tasks, using technology, and partnering with others magnify output. One hour of expertise can become ten, one hundred, or more through networks and automation. Scalability is embedded in the system rather than the individual. Personal effort becomes optional over time.

Monetization strategies are central. Skills must generate value for others to produce financial returns. Pricing, distribution channels, and accessibility are part of the system. Without monetization, a skill remains potential rather than realized wealth. The goal is impact that produces enduring financial outcomes.

Skills can also compound with other assets. Knowledge applied in business ventures, investment decisions, or intellectual property grows alongside capital. Experience accelerates learning, systems multiply reach, and networks increase opportunities. Each element reinforces the others, creating a self-sustaining growth cycle.

Patience is key. Turning skills into scalable assets is rarely immediate. It requires initial investment, trial, and iteration. Early results may seem modest, but persistence compounds returns. Long-term thinking ensures that effort today produces exponential benefit tomorrow.

Ultimately, scalable skill assets bridge effort and freedom. They free the individual from time-bound labor while creating persistent value. Skills cease to be merely a source of income; they become engines of wealth, influence, and optionality. Mastery is measured not by hours worked, but by impact multiplied across systems and time.

Chapter .20

Automating Progress to Remove Willpower

Systems succeed because they function even when motivation fails.

One of the biggest barriers to wealth creation is reliance on willpower. Motivation fluctuates, energy wanes, and discipline is tested daily. Relying solely on personal effort to achieve financial goals is fragile and unsustainable. The solution is automation: designing systems that continue to function regardless of momentary motivation. Automation converts consistency into compounding progress.

Automation begins with processes. Repetitive tasks are prime candidates for systemization. Bill payments, investment contributions, and routine business operations can all be automated. By removing human intervention, errors decrease, and output becomes predictable. What once required constant attention now operates independently, freeing both time and mental energy.

Behavioral automation is equally powerful. Habits, routines, and decision frameworks can be structured to produce consistent results. For example, allocating a fixed percentage of income to investments or scheduling time for skill-building removes the need for constant decision-making. Systems enforce discipline so that progress occurs naturally.

Financial automation also leverages technology. Software, apps, and platforms streamline operations, track metrics, and optimize efficiency. Automation reduces friction and increases reliability. It transforms scattered effort into a cohesive engine of growth. Even when motivation fades, systems continue producing results.

Delegation is another form of automation. Assigning tasks to trusted team members or collaborators allows scale beyond individual effort. Work is multiplied while personal energy is preserved. This approach converts human capital into leverage, amplifying both productivity and impact. Systems function independently of single individuals.

Automation also mitigates procrastination and distraction. By predefining processes and triggers, decisions are removed from moments of temptation or fatigue. Momentum becomes automatic. The energy previously spent resisting distraction is redirected toward strategic growth. Effort is concentrated where it produces the highest return.

A well-automated system is self-correcting. Monitoring, feedback loops, and contingency plans ensure that progress continues despite unexpected events. Systems adapt to changing conditions without requiring constant human intervention. This resilience preserves gains and protects against setbacks. Reliability is embedded.

Automation extends to learning and personal growth. Scheduling deliberate practice, using tools for efficiency, and creating repeatable study frameworks ensure skills compound over time. Knowledge becomes durable and accessible. Growth continues even during periods of low motivation, maintaining long-term trajectory.

The psychological benefit is profound. When systems are automated, stress decreases, focus improves, and confidence grows. Motivation becomes optional rather than mandatory. This frees mental bandwidth to engage in strategic thinking, creativity, and opportunity-seeking. Energy is redirected from maintenance to creation.

Ultimately, automating progress converts effort into systems, habits, and processes that function independently of willpower. Wealth becomes predictable rather than precarious. Consistency replaces chaos, and compounding replaces linear effort. Motivation is no longer the bottleneck; systems carry the work forward even when human energy falters.

PART V: LEVERAGE, SCALE, AND OWNERSHIP

Chapter .21

Why Ownership Beats Participation

Equity compounds while wages expire.

Participation, in the form of employment or contract work, exchanges time for income. It is linear and finite: each hour worked produces a fixed reward. Ownership, by contrast, allows value creation beyond personal effort. Equity in a business, intellectual property, or investment generates returns that compound over time. While wages stop when work ends, ownership continues to produce, multiplying impact and financial freedom.

Ownership aligns incentives with outcomes. Owners benefit from the growth and efficiency of the systems they control. Their upside is theoretically unlimited, whereas participants are capped by contracts or salaries. This asymmetry explains why wealth accumulates disproportionately among owners, even when their initial effort is similar to that of employees.

Equity compounds in multiple ways. Financially, it generates returns through appreciation, dividends, or revenue sharing. Strategically, it attracts leverage: additional capital, talent, and partnerships. Socially, it provides influence and opportunities that wage-based participation rarely affords. The compounding effect of ownership is exponential, unlike the linear accumulation of income.

Participation often limits freedom. Participants rely on external validation, schedules, and approvals. Decisions about career or financial strategy are constrained by hierarchy or policy. Owners control outcomes, resources, and direction. This control transforms risk into opportunity. Optionality is embedded, allowing owners to pivot, scale, or innovate without external permission.

Ownership is not without responsibility. Risk, accountability, and complexity increase as control grows. Owners must manage capital, people, and operations effectively. Yet these challenges are surmountable and are often accompanied by disproportionately greater rewards. The trade-off between effort and outcome favors those who embrace ownership despite initial difficulty.

The mindset shift is critical. Participants focus on tasks, efficiency, and compliance. Owners focus on growth, leverage, and system design. Decisions are evaluated for long-term compounding impact rather than short-term execution. This reorientation allows one to build assets that operate independently of direct effort.

Ownership amplifies wealth creation by allowing others' work to contribute to your results. Delegated labor, automated systems, and strategic investments all produce value that does not require constant input. One hour of ownership-focused action can generate decades of returns. This magnifies both effort and financial resilience.

Participation may feel safe, but it is ultimately fragile. Employment income is finite, dependent on continued performance or external factors. Ownership provides a structural advantage: assets, systems, and equity continue producing value under varying conditions. Security is embedded in control, not in permission or paychecks.

Building ownership also encourages strategic patience. Growth often requires delayed gratification, reinvestment, and calculated risk. Unlike participation, which rewards immediate output, ownership compounds with time. The earlier one acquires and nurtures equity, the greater the eventual benefit.

Ultimately, wealth accumulation is far more effective when structured around ownership rather than participation. Wages may provide comfort, but they cannot generate optionality, compounding, or freedom. Equity multiplies; wages expire. Recognizing this distinction is foundational to creating systems that generate durable wealth.

Reflection

Early in my career, I treated ownership as optional and participation as sufficient. Over time, I realized that the compounding power of equity far exceeded any linear wage. Embracing ownership—despite its responsibilities—transformed my trajectory, creating leverage and optionality I never experienced as a participant.

"Equity compounds; wages expire. Choose control over comfort."
— Naval Ravikant

Chapter .22

Using Other People's Time Without Exploiting It

Ethical leverage creates win-win outcomes at scale.

Leverage is most powerful when it involves multiplying effort through other people's time and skills. However, unethical approaches exploit labor, creating short-term gain at the expense of trust, morale, and sustainability. True wealth is generated when other people's time is leveraged ethically, producing benefits for both parties. This approach transforms collaboration into compounding value rather than exploitation.

Ethical leverage begins with respect. Those whose time is being utilized must feel valued, fairly compensated, and aligned with shared goals. Clear expectations, incentives, and accountability create trust. When people understand how their contribution advances both their interest and the system's goals, engagement multiplies. Motivation is embedded rather than forced.

Delegation is the foundation of leveraging time. Routine, repetitive, or specialized tasks can be assigned to others while focusing on higher-level strategy and creation. Proper delegation maximizes efficiency without diminishing quality. It also frees mental bandwidth for decisions that only the owner or system architect can make. The key is designing roles that empower rather than constrain.

Leverage also includes mentorship and skill amplification. Teaching others to perform tasks, create systems, or innovate extends capability far beyond personal limits. Each trained individual becomes a multiplier, producing value independently while contributing to the broader system. Knowledge and guidance compound similarly to financial assets.

Technology amplifies ethical leverage further. Automation, platforms, and collaboration tools allow one person's decisions to affect many. Processes, content, and systems replicate effort without constant oversight. The ethical principle remains: these tools enhance outcomes without diminishing fairness or transparency. Scale becomes sustainable, not exploitative.

Transparency and communication are critical. Leveraged relationships must be mutually understood and aligned. Misaligned incentives lead to resentment, inefficiency, or attrition. Ethical leverage is self-reinforcing: trust breeds loyalty, skill-building multiplies value, and aligned incentives accelerate system growth. Exploitation, by contrast, collapses over time.

Ethical leverage also includes proper compensation structures. Performance-based incentives, profit-sharing, and ownership stakes ensure contributors benefit from the success of the system. When gains are shared proportionally, motivation and collaboration increase. Systems outperform because human capital is energized rather than drained.

The mindset shift is essential. Leverage is not about doing less work at someone else's expense; it is about multiplying collective effort through alignment, empowerment, and systems. Time and energy are treated as precious resources, deployed thoughtfully to maximize impact while preserving ethical standards. Wealth is generated without compromising integrity.

Ethical leverage creates scalability. As trust, competence, and systems multiply, one individual can influence outcomes far beyond personal capacity. Each layer of the system reinforces the other, creating compounding growth. The effect is long-term and self-sustaining. Exploitation may offer short-term gain, but only ethical leverage produces durable wealth.

Ultimately, leveraging other people's time ethically transforms systems, productivity, and wealth. It turns labor into a force multiplier while building trust, loyalty, and capability. Ethical leverage aligns human effort with strategic objectives, creating compounding results that benefit all participants. Wealth is no longer limited by individual effort—it becomes collective, scalable, and sustainable.

Reflection

I learned early that trying to do everything myself limited both scale and growth. Initially, I struggled to delegate without feeling I was burdening others. Once I focused on ethical leverage, empowering people and aligning incentives, productivity soared. Collaboration became a force multiplier, and wealth creation accelerated without compromising integrity.

"Ethical leverage is the multiplier that creates sustainable wealth."
— Unknown

CHAPTER .23

CAPITAL AS A TOOL, NOT A TROPHY

Money works best when deployed strategically, not hoarded emotionally.

Many people view capital as a symbol of success rather than a means to generate more value. Savings without purpose, idle investments, or excessive accumulation can feel safe but often fail to create wealth. Capital becomes powerful only when used strategically as a tool to build systems, scale operations, or generate passive income. The key is distinguishing between money as a resource and money as a status symbol.

Capital functions like fuel for wealth-building engines. It can acquire assets, leverage opportunities, and create additional revenue streams. Holding capital without deployment is like storing energy without connecting it to a generator. Growth is dependent on active use: investing, lending, or deploying funds in systems that amplify returns. Strategic allocation is critical.

Hoarding capital often stems from fear. People worry about losing money, making the wrong decision, or experiencing volatility. While caution is necessary, excessive conservatism limits compounding and optionality. Capital's power is realized when it is put to work thoughtfully, balancing risk with potential reward. Deliberate action creates growth; inaction preserves only anxiety.

Capital deployed strategically can accelerate leverage. Investments, acquisitions, or partnerships enable one unit of money to generate multiple returns. The effects multiply when combined with systems, technology, and human capital. Unlike wages, which are linear, capital can compound exponentially, producing financial gravity over time.

Strategic use of capital also includes risk management. Diversification, hedging, and contingency planning preserve both principal and growth potential. Capital deployed intelligently supports resilience while enabling growth. The goal is to create asymmetrical outcomes: upside potential exceeds downside exposure. This mindset transforms money from a trophy into a tool for freedom.

Mindset shifts are required to treat capital as functional rather than emotional. Decisions are guided by opportunity, compounding potential, and alignment with long-term goals. Emotional attachment leads to hoarding or impulsive spending, while strategic thinking maximizes returns. Discipline ensures that capital continues to serve purpose, not ego.

Capital can also enable access to other forms of leverage. Financial resources attract talent, partnerships, and opportunities that would otherwise be unavailable. It becomes a tool to acquire time, skills, and influence. Deployed properly, it multiplies not just wealth but strategic capacity.

The difference between money as a trophy and a tool is evident in behavior. Those who hoard may appear wealthy but lack optionality. Those who deploy wisely may not flaunt their resources but achieve lasting independence and influence. Wealth is measured by flexibility, scalability, and impact, not by raw accumulation.

Finally, viewing capital as a tool encourages experimentation. Risk-managed deployment allows testing new ideas, entering markets, and creating systems that compound over time. Each strategic decision reinforces learning and positions resources for maximum growth. Capital becomes an engine rather than a trophy.

Ultimately, wealth multiplies when money is treated as a tool for strategic growth rather than a symbol of achievement. Deployment creates opportunity, leverage, and optionality. Hoarding creates security illusions but limits freedom. Understanding this principle transforms not only finances but also mindset and outcomes.

Chapter .24

Technology as a Wealth Multiplier

Digital systems allow small teams to create massive impact.

Technology has transformed the landscape of wealth creation. Unlike linear effort, digital tools allow a small input to generate exponential outcomes. One person or a small team can reach millions, automate processes, and scale operations globally. Understanding how to harness technology multiplies both productivity and financial impact, making it a cornerstone of modern wealth systems.

Automation is one of the most powerful applications of technology. Repetitive tasks, data management, and customer interactions can be managed by software, freeing human effort for higher-level strategy. Systems operate continuously without fatigue, creating consistency and reliability. This allows time and energy to be redirected toward tasks that cannot be automated.

Platforms amplify reach. Online marketplaces, social networks, and distribution channels provide access to audiences far beyond physical limitations. A single product, service, or piece of content can be replicated and delivered at scale. Impact is no longer limited by geography or personal labor, turning effort into compounding opportunity.

Technology also enables leverage of capital and human resources. Tools, applications, and systems allow smaller teams to outperform much larger organizations. Efficiency, precision, and speed are enhanced, and barriers to entry are reduced. Entrepreneurs and builders can create significant value with minimal initial resources, accelerating wealth accumulation.

Data and analytics multiply intelligence. Insights gathered through digital tools inform strategic decisions, optimize processes, and predict trends. This reduces uncertainty and increases the probability of successful outcomes. Systems that adapt to information grow faster, creating both operational and financial leverage.

Technology can also create passive revenue streams. Software, digital content, automated services, and online courses generate income long after the initial work is done. These assets scale independently of direct effort. Combining technology with ethical leverage and strategic capital magnifies returns, producing durable financial gravity.

The mindset shift is critical. Technology should be viewed as an amplifier, not a distraction. Tools are selected and implemented based on their ability to multiply impact, reduce friction, and expand reach. Random adoption or novelty-focused use produces little wealth. Systems thinking ensures technology works as part of a larger compounding framework.

Risks must be managed. Overreliance, misalignment, or poor integration can undermine results. Security, scalability, and sustainability are priorities. Effective implementation requires planning, oversight, and regular optimization. Technology becomes a reliable partner rather than a liability.

Collaboration is enhanced through tech. Distributed teams, cloud systems, and communication platforms allow coordination across time zones and specialties. Skills and knowledge are shared, scaled, and reinforced. Collective output is amplified far beyond what individuals alone could achieve, creating compounding impact.

Ultimately, technology is a force multiplier for wealth creation. It amplifies labor, capital, and systems. It enables scale, efficiency, and global reach. When leveraged ethically and strategically, technology allows small teams or individuals to achieve massive outcomes, turning effort into enduring wealth.

Reflection

Initially, I underestimated the power of technology, seeing it as a convenience rather than a multiplier. Once I began designing systems, automating processes, and leveraging platforms, the scale of what was possible expanded dramatically. Technology became the engine that amplified my efforts, creating wealth far beyond what I could achieve manually.

"Technology is the lever that multiplies effort exponentially."
— Naval Ravikant

CHAPTER .25

BUILDING ONCE AND GETTING PAID REPEATEDLY

Recurring value is the foundation of durable wealth.

One of the most powerful principles in wealth creation is designing systems or products that generate recurring returns. Instead of exchanging time for money, assets are structured to continue producing value long after the initial effort. Whether through intellectual property, subscriptions, or scalable services, building once and getting paid repeatedly multiplies impact and accelerates financial freedom.

The concept begins with leverage. Traditional work ties income directly to hours or effort. Recurring systems decouple value from time. A single creation—a course, software, or content—can reach thousands of people, generating income continuously. This creates compounding returns that scale far beyond manual labor.

Products and services with recurring revenue are particularly effective. Subscription models, licensing, and automated solutions provide predictable cash flow. The system produces income continuously without repeated labor. This stability allows further investment in assets, skills, or leverage, amplifying the cycle of wealth creation.

Scalability is central. Once a system is built, marginal cost of additional delivery is minimal. Technology, automation, and distribution channels enable replication without significant extra effort. Each replication compounds value while freeing human energy for higher-level tasks. The initial investment multiplies over time.

Designing for recurrence also enhances resilience. Predictable systems provide a buffer against volatility. Dependence on active labor or one-off transactions introduces risk and fragility. Recurring assets create continuity, optionality, and financial gravity. The system itself becomes a durable engine of wealth.

Marketing and reach amplify the principle. Even the best system requires users, clients, or consumers. Building distribution and awareness ensures that value reaches those who can pay repeatedly. Leverage human networks, technology, and content channels to expand reach and maintain flow. Systems that scale are self-reinforcing.

Ethical value creation is key. Systems should deliver genuine benefit, service, or improvement. Repeatable revenue models succeed when users perceive ongoing value. Ethical design strengthens trust, reduces churn, and compounds both reputation and income. Impact and profitability reinforce each other.

Automation complements recurrence. Processes, communication, billing, and delivery can all be automated, reducing reliance on human input. Systems function continuously and reliably, minimizing friction and maximizing output. Automation converts labor into lasting compounding value.

The mindset shift is profound. Builders stop measuring work by hours and start measuring by system output. Effort is front-loaded, and rewards continue long after the initial input. One creation, carefully designed, can produce decades of income, influence, and freedom. This principle separates temporary earners from enduring wealth creators.

Ultimately, building once and getting paid repeatedly is the essence of system-based wealth. It transforms labor into leverage, ideas into assets, and effort into compounding impact. Recurring value is the foundation upon which scalable, durable, and autonomous wealth is built.

PART VI:
RISK, FAILURE, AND RESILIENCE

CHAPTER .26

WHY PLAYING IT SAFE IS THE RISKIEST STRATEGY

Avoiding risk often guarantees long-term financial vulnerability.

Most people equate safety with low risk. They stick to predictable paths, trade-offs, and investments, believing security is the absence of risk. Yet in wealth creation, avoiding risk entirely often ensures stagnation or decline. Inflation, market shifts, and technological disruption erode assets over time. True security requires calculated risk-taking and proactive positioning.

Playing it safe limits potential returns. Low-risk assets and predictable income streams rarely outpace inflation or create significant wealth. While they feel secure in the short term, they fail to leverage compounding and opportunity. Those who take thoughtful risks gain disproportionate rewards over time, creating freedom and optionality.

Risk assessment, rather than avoidance, is the differentiator. Calculated risks involve understanding the probability of success, potential consequences, and mitigation strategies. Risk-taking without preparation is reckless; risk avoidance without strategy is stagnation. Wealth is built when risk is recognized, analyzed, and strategically embraced.

Opportunities often reside where others fear to tread. Markets, ideas, and innovations carry inherent uncertainty. Early movers face discomfort, unpredictability, and potential setbacks. Those willing to navigate uncertainty, however, access outsized returns.

Playing it safe guarantees missing these opportunities while embracing risk strategically creates growth.

Risk is also about timing and scale. Diversified, incremental exposure allows experimentation while limiting downside. Leverage, systems, and contingency plans amplify gains while protecting against catastrophic loss. Playing it safe removes these options, leaving one dependent on finite income or depreciating assets.

The mindset of risk embraces failure as learning. Each calculated risk provides data, experience, and insight. Over time, pattern recognition and judgment improve. Avoiding risk leaves one ignorant of these lessons, unable to identify opportunities or threats. Growth stagnates in comfort zones.

Playing it safe often disguises fear as prudence. Comfort, routine, and predictability are seductive but costly over time. The illusion of security keeps people trapped in linear outcomes. Real wealth comes from balancing courage with strategy, recognizing that temporary discomfort is a prerequisite for lasting freedom.

Strategic risk is amplified by systems. Leverage, automation, and partnerships reduce exposure while magnifying upside. Risks taken within well-designed frameworks are calculated rather than blind. Systems allow experimentation with manageable consequences, creating optionality and resilience.

Ultimately, avoiding risk entirely is a passive strategy that undermines long-term wealth. Security is not the absence of risk but the control of it. Calculated risk-taking, combined with systems, leverage, and patience, creates freedom, optionality, and compounding outcomes. Those who embrace risk strategically thrive while the cautious remain stagnant.

CHAPTER .27

INTELLIGENT FAILURE AS TUITION

Mistakes become assets when lessons are captured and applied.

Failure is often feared and avoided, yet it is one of the most powerful teachers in wealth creation. Each setback, mistake, or misstep provides critical feedback about systems, strategy, and behavior. When approached intelligently, failure is not a loss but tuition—a payment for education that accelerates growth. Understanding this principle transforms the fear of failure into a tool for compounding success.

Intelligent failure requires reflection. After each setback, analyzing what went wrong, why it happened, and how to improve ensures that the lesson is captured. This process converts a negative experience into actionable knowledge. Repeating this cycle refines decision-making, strengthens systems, and enhances judgment over time.

Failure also signals experimentation. In wealth building, experimentation is necessary to identify scalable systems, leverage points, and asset opportunities. Not all experiments succeed, but each provides insight into what works and what does not. Fear of failure, by contrast, inhibits experimentation, leaving systems stagnant and potential unrealized.

The compounding effect of intelligent failure is profound. Each lesson learned informs future decisions, reducing the probability of repeated mistakes. Knowledge gained through experience accelerates growth, allowing one to navigate complexity with increasing efficiency. Mistakes become building blocks rather than obstacles.

Emotional resilience is another benefit. Experiencing and analyzing failure teaches patience, humility, and adaptability. Those who embrace lessons from failure develop the capacity to endure uncertainty and discomfort. Emotional control becomes a system in itself, reinforcing rational decision-making under stress.

Intelligent failure is also about minimizing unnecessary loss. Calculated experiments, contingency planning, and risk management ensure that lessons are learned without catastrophic consequences. Systems capture knowledge and prevent repeated errors, transforming setbacks into structured growth opportunities. This is tuition that compounds rather than drains.

Collaboration amplifies the learning from failure. Sharing insights with teams, mentors, or partners multiplies the benefit of each lesson. Others can avoid pitfalls, optimize strategies, and contribute additional perspectives. Failure, when shared intelligently, becomes a collective accelerator for systems and wealth creation.

The mindset shift is crucial. Viewing failure as tuition requires reframing outcomes. Losses are temporary, feedback is valuable, and long-term compounding is the goal. Those who internalize this perspective act decisively, iterate quickly, and avoid paralysis by fear. Progress is exponential when every mistake is leveraged.

Ultimately, intelligent failure is a strategic asset. It converts setbacks into education, risk into insight, and mistakes into compounding knowledge. Systems improve, judgment sharpens, and resilience strengthens. Wealth is built not despite failure, but because it is approached as tuition for mastery.

CHAPTER .28

ANTI-FRAGILE WEALTH SYSTEMS

The strongest systems improve under stress instead of collapsing.

Traditional financial systems are fragile: they perform well under normal conditions but break under stress. Anti-fragile systems, by contrast, gain strength from volatility, shocks, and adversity. Wealth built through anti-fragile structures not only survives uncertainty but thrives in its presence. This concept transforms risk from a threat into a growth opportunity.

Anti-fragility begins with diversity. Assets, revenue streams, and systems that are spread across different domains, markets, and instruments are less vulnerable to single points of failure. When one element is stressed, others compensate or benefit. Redundancy and strategic distribution create resilience that compounds over time.

Optionality is another key principle. Anti-fragile systems maintain flexibility to capitalize on unexpected opportunities. They are not rigid or over-leveraged, allowing swift adaptation when conditions change. The capacity to pivot ensures that stress does not produce collapse but opens avenues for growth.

Stress testing enhances anti-fragility. Systems should be regularly challenged with simulated scenarios, worst-case analyses, and deliberate exposure to volatility. This identifies weaknesses, refines processes, and prepares for real-world shocks. The system becomes stronger with each challenge, much like muscles growing through resistance.

Leverage must be carefully managed. While borrowed capital, human resources, and technology can amplify returns, excessive exposure increases fragility. Anti-fragile systems use leverage strategically, ensuring it enhances rather than endangers growth. Controlled amplification allows stress to become constructive rather than destructive.

Feedback loops strengthen systems further. Rapid detection of errors, inefficiencies, or vulnerabilities allows quick adaptation. Continuous learning and iteration ensure that the system evolves with environmental changes. Wealth systems that are static eventually weaken, while adaptive systems compound in strength and durability.

Psychological anti-fragility is also critical. Builders develop resilience, patience, and perspective, allowing them to act decisively under stress. Emotional responses are managed, reducing the likelihood of reactionary decisions. The combination of structural and personal anti-fragility ensures sustainable growth even in volatility.

Anti-fragile systems also benefit from decentralization. Decision-making, resources, and production are distributed to avoid catastrophic failure. Diverse contributors, markets, or assets provide multiple pathways for success. The system thrives when individual elements encounter stress, as adaptation produces overall gains.

Finally, anti-fragile wealth is not about avoiding shocks; it is about embracing and benefiting from them. Systems are intentionally designed to improve with each challenge, turning uncertainty into a catalyst for growth. Wealth compounds not despite adversity, but because it has been structured to exploit it.

Ultimately, creating anti-fragile wealth systems ensures that progress is durable, scalable, and resilient. Risk, volatility, and change are transformed into advantages rather than threats. These systems grow stronger with time, stress, and experimentation, producing compounding freedom and optionality.

REFLECTION:

I used to fear market volatility and life's uncertainties, building systems that were fragile under stress. When I began designing anti-fragile structures—diverse, flexible, and adaptive—I discovered that challenges no longer threatened my trajectory. Each disruption became an opportunity to strengthen my wealth systems.

"Stress tests reveal weakness, adaptation creates strength." — James Clear

Chapter .29

Protecting the Downside Without Limiting the Upside

Smart risk management preserves growth while preventing ruin.

Wealth creation is a balance between opportunity and protection. Focusing solely on growth exposes one to catastrophic loss, while excessive caution stifles potential. Protecting the downside while preserving the upside is the hallmark of intelligent financial strategy. It allows compounding, experimentation, and leverage without risking irreparable harm.

Downside protection begins with risk identification. Assets, systems, and investments are analyzed for potential failure points, market volatility, and structural vulnerabilities. Contingency plans are created to mitigate losses. By knowing where exposure exists, one can act preemptively rather than reactively, ensuring stability during turbulent periods.

Diversification is a critical strategy. Spreading capital across different asset types, industries, and geographies reduces dependency on any single factor. A downturn in one area is offset by stability or growth in others. Diversification preserves optionality, allowing upside opportunities to continue compounding without being derailed by isolated risks.

Hedging and insurance further protect against catastrophic loss. Financial instruments, contracts, and policies act as buffers, absorbing shocks without impeding growth. These tools convert unpredictable events into manageable scenarios, ensuring that experimentation and leverage do not threaten the system. Protection becomes a strategic enabler.

Flexibility enhances resilience. Systems should be designed to adapt quickly to market shifts, disruptions, or mistakes. Liquidity, scalable operations, and contingency protocols allow for quick pivots without destroying value. Optionality ensures that upside is never fully sacrificed while downside risks are controlled.

Emotional discipline supports downside protection. Fear can lead to overreaction, while greed can create reckless exposure. Maintaining a rational, long-term perspective ensures that actions reinforce both security and growth. Decisions are guided by data, systems, and strategic principles rather than impulses.

Leverage must be managed carefully. Strategic use of capital, human resources, and technology multiplies returns, but over-leverage increases fragility. Protecting the downside involves ensuring that leverage is employed in a controlled and calculated manner. This enables the upside to compound without threatening the foundation.

Scenario planning strengthens decision-making. Simulating extreme cases, stress testing assets, and anticipating black swan events allow systems to endure unforeseen shocks. By preparing for worst-case scenarios, the probability of catastrophic failure decreases, and opportunities for upside remain accessible.

Ultimately, protecting the downside without limiting the upside requires an integrated approach: diversified assets, hedging, flexibility, leverage management, and disciplined psychology. Wealth grows steadily and sustainably, insulated from ruin while poised for compounding growth. This strategy transforms uncertainty into opportunity rather than risk.

Reflection

I used to equate safety with low risk, often sacrificing growth to avoid discomfort. Learning to protect the downside while preserving upside allowed me to take calculated risks confidently. My systems could experiment, leverage, and compound without fear of collapse, making progress both durable and exponential.

"Smart systems grow because they survive the shocks others fear."
— James Clear

Chapter .30

Redefining Security in an Unstable World

True security comes from adaptability, not guarantees.

Traditional notions of financial security rely on fixed income, predictable schedules, and guaranteed outcomes. In an increasingly volatile world, these guarantees are illusions. Economic shifts, technological disruption, and global instability render rigid systems fragile. True security is not the absence of risk but the ability to adapt, respond, and thrive under changing conditions.

Adaptability begins with mindset. Builders cultivate flexibility, curiosity, and resilience. They view challenges as opportunities and uncertainty as optionality. Security is internalized through skills, knowledge, and strategic systems rather than external guarantees. The ability to pivot quickly becomes the cornerstone of durable wealth.

Financial systems must be designed for agility. Diversified assets, scalable operations, and flexible cash flow provide the capacity to respond to unexpected events. Fixed commitments are balanced with liquid resources, allowing rapid adaptation. Security emerges not from stasis but from the capacity to adjust without losing momentum.

Skills and human capital are vital components of security. Knowledge, networks, and experience create a buffer against instability. When markets or systems shift, transferable skills provide both income and leverage. Investing in oneself ensures that adaptability is not hypothetical but actionable.

Redundancy strengthens resilience. Multiple streams of income, alternative investments, and fallback plans create structural stability. Redundancy does not equate to inefficiency; instead, it enables continuity while maintaining optionality. When one system falters, others compensate, preserving both progress and freedom.

Embracing uncertainty is a mindset shift. Rather than fearing volatility, adaptable builders anticipate it, positioning themselves to capitalize on change. Opportunities often emerge in periods of disruption. Security becomes proactive rather than reactive, transforming chaos into compounding advantage.

Technology and systems amplify adaptability. Automation, platforms, and process design reduce dependency on fragile human execution. Systems function under stress and adapt to evolving conditions, allowing human attention to focus on strategic opportunities. Security is embedded within these resilient structures.

Flexibility in lifestyle and spending further reinforces security. Avoiding over-leverage, maintaining liquidity, and living below means ensure that personal systems can absorb shocks. Behavioral discipline complements structural resilience, creating a comprehensive approach to security.

Ultimately, security is redefined as the capacity to adapt rather than the expectation of certainty. Wealth is preserved and grows when systems, skills, and mindset are resilient to change. In an unstable world, adaptability becomes the ultimate currency, providing freedom, opportunity, and durable financial stability.

PART VII: WEALTH AS A LIFESTYLE SYSTEM

Chapter .31

Designing Life Around Freedom, Not Income

Wealth should support life choices, not consume them.

Most people pursue wealth as if income is the ultimate goal, forgetting that financial resources exist to create freedom. True wealth allows control over time, priorities, and lifestyle rather than forcing life to revolve around earning. Designing life around freedom shifts focus from reactive labor to intentional creation of systems, assets, and choices that serve long-term fulfillment.

Freedom-first design starts with clarity on values and priorities. What experiences, relationships, and contributions matter most? Understanding these allows financial systems to align with personal objectives. Income becomes a tool to support these goals, not a substitute for meaning. Life is structured intentionally rather than dictated by necessity.

Time is the most valuable currency. By building systems that generate passive income and scalable assets, individuals reclaim hours and days from labor. Freedom-first design prioritizes efficiency, leverage, and automation. Every financial decision is evaluated for its impact on time, freedom, and long-term optionality.

Lifestyle planning is integral. Choices about where to live, how to spend, and what to pursue are informed by freedom rather than obligations. Wealth is used to enhance life, not to enable endless consumption or vanity. Frugality, investment, and strategic allocation of resources preserve optionality while maximizing satisfaction.

Systems are designed to support flexibility. Income streams, investments, and work obligations are structured to allow pivots, experimentation, and opportunities. Overcommitment to rigid schedules or hierarchical employment reduces freedom. Wealth systems must be adaptable to support a life centered on choice.

The mindset shift is crucial. Builders prioritize freedom over status, autonomy over accumulation, and optionality over short-term comfort. Income is a means, not an end. This perspective encourages decisions that compound long-term well-being rather than satisfy immediate desire.

Relationships and community are also aligned with freedom-first design. Social capital, mentorship, and collaboration enhance both wealth and quality of life. Time spent nurturing meaningful connections is considered an investment, not a cost. The system supports both financial and human capital growth.

Risk management complements freedom. Safeguards, redundancy, and optionality prevent life choices from being constrained by unexpected events. Strategic planning ensures that freedom is durable, not fragile. Wealth is insulated from shocks that could force compromise on lifestyle or values.

Ultimately, designing life around freedom transforms wealth from a goal into a tool. Income, assets, and systems are leveraged to create time, autonomy, and optionality. Life becomes intentionally directed, with financial resources serving choice rather than compulsion. Freedom-first thinking ensures wealth is enduring and meaningful.

Chapter .32

Time as the Ultimate Currency

Financial systems exist to reclaim control over your time.

Time is the only truly non-renewable resource, yet most people treat it as expendable. Traditional income models trade hours for dollars, creating a linear and finite relationship between effort and reward. Recognizing time as the ultimate currency shifts focus from earning more to designing systems, assets, and leverage that maximize freedom and optionality.

The first step is measuring time value. Understanding how much each hour contributes to both immediate income and long-term wealth allows prioritization. Some tasks should be automated, delegated, or eliminated entirely. This creates leverage, freeing energy for high-impact activities that cannot be replicated by others.

Passive income transforms time into a compounding asset. Systems that generate recurring revenue, royalties, or residuals decouple financial returns from personal labor. Time invested once can yield benefits for decades. Viewing money as a means to reclaim time rather than an end in itself creates a strategic framework for financial decisions.

Leverage accelerates the compounding of time. By using other people's labor, technology, and capital, one hour of effort can produce results far beyond its immediate contribution. Systems, automation, and scalable assets multiply time's impact. Each hour saved becomes an investment in freedom and optionality.

Time management becomes a strategic skill. Allocating hours according to value rather than urgency ensures that energy compounds instead of dissipates. Avoiding time-wasting activities and prioritizing long-term growth over short-term comfort is essential. Wealth without time freedom is hollow and unsustainable.

Lifestyle design complements time-focused systems. Reducing unnecessary commitments, minimizing distractions, and structuring environments to preserve autonomy enhances the value of wealth. Time saved through efficient systems, delegation, and automation is reinvested in experiences, relationships, and growth, maximizing life satisfaction.

Risk management protects time as well as money. Illiquidity, overcommitment, and dependence on fragile income sources threaten both freedom and financial security. Diversification of income streams and creation of durable systems ensures that time remains under control even under stress. Optionality is preserved for future choices.

Time-centered thinking also shifts mindset. Success is measured not by salary, possessions, or appearances, but by hours gained, freedom maintained, and opportunities created. Wealth is a tool to purchase experiences, autonomy, and influence. Decisions prioritize longevity and quality of life over immediate gratification.

Ultimately, treating time as the ultimate currency changes every aspect of wealth creation. Systems, leverage, and automation transform finite hours into compounding freedom. Money becomes a servant to time, rather than the master, and life becomes intentionally directed rather than dictated by circumstance.

CHAPTER .33

AVOIDING LIFESTYLE INFLATION TRAPS

Growing expenses silently destroy growing income.

As income increases, many people unconsciously expand their lifestyle to match, creating what is known as lifestyle inflation. Higher earnings are often absorbed by larger bills, upgraded conveniences, and social expectations. This pattern can silently sabotage wealth accumulation, as gains are immediately consumed rather than deployed into systems, assets, or compounding growth.

Lifestyle inflation often feels rewarding in the short term. New cars, bigger homes, or luxurious experiences provide immediate satisfaction. Yet these incremental upgrades rarely contribute to long-term freedom. Money that could have been invested, leveraged, or automated instead becomes a liability that grows alongside income.

Awareness is the first defense. Tracking expenses, evaluating purchases against long-term goals, and distinguishing needs from wants allows conscious decision-making. Every dollar should be assessed for its impact on wealth creation rather than momentary pleasure. Discipline preserves optionality and ensures financial growth continues unabated.

Automation and systems can counteract lifestyle creep. Automatically allocating a fixed percentage of income toward investments, scalable assets, or savings ensures that money is working for growth before lifestyle desires claim it. This "pay yourself first" approach enforces compounding and prevents consumption from undermining wealth.

The mindset shift is crucial. Wealth builders prioritize freedom and optionality over status or appearances. Delaying gratification and maintaining consistency in spending allows assets to compound over time. Lifestyle becomes a choice aligned with purpose rather than an automatic consequence of higher income.

Social pressures exacerbate lifestyle inflation. Comparing oneself to peers, family, or societal standards often drives spending that erodes financial goals. Building awareness of external influences and creating personal benchmarks helps maintain control over resources. True freedom comes from aligning expenditure with values, not expectations.

Reinvestment creates resilience. Money preserved and directed into growth generates future optionality. Avoiding lifestyle inflation ensures that income increases translate into enhanced freedom rather than additional obligations. Compounding becomes the dominant force rather than being neutralized by consumption.

Frugality and intentional living are not deprivation; they are strategic tools. Choosing high-value experiences, prioritizing long-term gains, and being conscious of trade-offs maintains wealth momentum. The balance between enjoyment and preservation is essential for sustainable progress.

Ultimately, avoiding lifestyle inflation is foundational for system-based wealth. Income growth is meaningless if it is consumed as fast as it is earned. Disciplined spending, automated allocation, and conscious prioritization of resources ensure that money fuels freedom, optionality, and durable wealth.

CHAPTER .34

TEACHING WEALTH THINKING TO THE NEXT GENERATION

Systems are more valuable when they outlive their creator.

Wealth is not merely financial; it is a mindset and a system of principles that can be passed down. Teaching the next generation to think in terms of assets, leverage, and scalable systems ensures that value compounds beyond a single lifetime. Education in wealth creation transforms inheritance from money alone into enduring freedom and optionality.

Begin with foundational concepts. Children and mentees should understand the difference between income and wealth, consumption versus construction, and linear effort versus systems-based growth. These lessons provide a framework for decisions that compound over time rather than dissipate potential through habits and reactive choices.

Modeling behavior is crucial. Systems thinking is absorbed more through observation than instruction. Demonstrating discipline, automation, strategic risk-taking, and ethical leverage instills practical understanding. Young people see not just theory but actionable implementation that they can emulate and adapt to their own lives.

Encourage ownership and experimentation. Allowing the next generation to make decisions, manage small projects, or invest resources provides hands-on experience. Intelligent failure and feedback teach lessons faster than abstract concepts. Systems, once tested, reinforce learning and produce compounding understanding.

Teach adaptability and optionality. The future is uncertain, and static rules rarely survive. By instilling flexibility, resilience, and the ability to pivot, you equip learners with the tools to thrive in volatile environments. Systems-based thinking is not rigid; it is designed to evolve and scale with circumstances.

Introduce the concept of compounding impact. Decisions made today, habits formed, and systems created can multiply over decades. The focus shifts from immediate gain to long-term strategic advantage. Understanding the exponential nature of wealth encourages patience, intentionality, and disciplined execution.

Integrate values with financial systems. Wealth thinking is not solely about money—it is about freedom, influence, and legacy. Teaching ethical leverage, responsible risk-taking, and meaningful impact ensures that compounding wealth benefits both the individual and the community. Systems outlive creators when grounded in purpose.

Practical tools support education. Budgeting frameworks, investment exercises, and entrepreneurial projects allow young learners to experience the principles firsthand. Combining theory with practice ensures that knowledge is internalized and becomes actionable. Repetition and iteration embed systems thinking deeply.

Ultimately, teaching wealth thinking creates legacy. It ensures that knowledge, systems, and values compound across generations. True wealth is measured not by money alone but by the freedom, optionality, and impact passed on. Systems that educate and empower multiply influence and opportunity far beyond the lifespan of their creator.

Chapter .35

Aligning Health, Energy, and Wealth

A broken body undermines even the best financial system.

Financial systems are only as effective as the people who operate them. Wealth without health is fragile because illness, fatigue, and poor energy management reduce productivity, decision-making ability, and capacity to leverage time. Aligning physical, mental, and emotional well-being with wealth-building systems ensures sustainable performance and long-term freedom.

Health fuels energy, and energy drives execution. High-functioning bodies and minds enable consistent action, focus, and creativity. Exercise, nutrition, sleep, and recovery are investments in the human capital that underpins financial systems. Without this foundation, even the most sophisticated systems struggle to operate efficiently.

Mental clarity is equally important. Stress management, mindfulness, and cognitive resilience support decision-making and strategic thinking. Fatigue and emotional imbalance distort judgment, increase mistakes, and reduce the ability to leverage opportunities. Healthy routines and practices amplify both speed and quality of wealth creation.

Energy management impacts leverage. High energy allows ethical delegation, mentoring, and system oversight to occur effectively. Low energy leads to micromanagement, delayed action, and reliance on suboptimal choices. Wealth multiplies when human capital is operating at full potential, enabling systems to scale and sustain performance.

Prevention is a form of wealth preservation. Chronic illness, burnout, or poor habits can create financial liabilities through lost time, medical costs, or reduced capacity. Investing in health reduces risk and ensures that other wealth systems function without interruption. Proactive care compounds over years, just like financial assets.

Lifestyle alignment matters. Time allocated to work, exercise, rest, and personal pursuits should be structured intentionally. Overemphasis on earning at the expense of health leads to diminishing returns. Balanced systems optimize both energy and financial output, ensuring sustainable wealth accumulation.

Synergy between mind and body enhances creativity. Healthy individuals generate better ideas, solve problems faster, and innovate within their systems. Physical vitality supports mental resilience, reinforcing both personal and financial growth. This creates a feedback loop where health amplifies wealth and vice versa.

Habits compound over time. Small daily practices in nutrition, movement, and mental fitness yield exponential results across decades. Neglecting these habits erodes long-term capacity to execute systems effectively. Consistency in self-care is as essential as consistency in financial systems.

Ultimately, health, energy, and wealth are inseparable. True financial freedom is unattainable without the human capital to operate, innovate, and leverage systems. Investing in well-being ensures that financial systems function optimally, enabling wealth, time freedom, and impact to compound sustainably.

PART VIII:
EXECUTION AND LEGACY

Chapter .36

Simplifying Wealth So It Actually Works

Complexity kills consistency, while simplicity compounds.

Wealth systems often fail not because of poor strategy, but because they are unnecessarily complex. Overly intricate plans, multiple accounts, convoluted investments, or elaborate rules create friction, confusion, and errors. Simplifying processes ensures consistent execution, reduces stress, and allows compounding to function unhindered over time.

Clarity begins with goals. Define what wealth means personally—freedom, optionality, impact—and design systems that directly support those outcomes. Avoid distraction from shiny objects or complicated strategies that do not align with objectives. Simplicity allows focus on what truly drives results.

Automation reduces complexity. By automating investments, bill payments, and routine operations, the system functions without constant human intervention. Fewer decisions reduce errors and decision fatigue. When execution is consistent, compounding and growth become reliable.

Prioritize high-leverage actions. Not all tasks contribute equally to wealth creation. Identify activities, investments, and habits that produce the greatest return per effort. Eliminating low-value complexity frees time, energy, and resources for high-impact actions, accelerating compounding and scaling.

Simplify communication and relationships in systems. Delegation, clear roles, and structured processes reduce misalignment and inefficiency. Whether in business, partnerships, or financial management, simplicity enhances transparency, accountability, and adaptability.

Decision frameworks further enhance simplicity. Predefined criteria for investing, spending, or scaling reduce indecision and emotional reactions. Rules-based approaches prevent over complication and maintain focus on outcomes. Simplicity ensures that decisions are aligned with long-term objectives rather than short-term impulses.

Monitoring and adjustment should also be streamlined. Metrics, dashboards, and feedback loops must be clear, actionable, and relevant. Excessive complexity in tracking erodes consistency and creates paralysis. Simplicity in evaluation allows the system to evolve efficiently.

The mindset shift is critical. Simplicity is not about doing less; it is about focusing on what matters most and removing friction. Wealth grows when systems are easy to understand, execute, and replicate. Complexity may impress others, but simplicity ensures effectiveness and sustainability.

Ultimately, wealth works best when it is simple. Systems that are easy to implement, automate, and maintain allow compounding to operate naturally. Clarity, focus, and streamlined processes transform effort into durable, scalable, and autonomous wealth creation.

Chapter .37

Measuring Progress Beyond Net Worth

True success includes freedom, resilience, and fulfillment.

Net worth is a common measure of wealth, but it tells only part of the story. True financial success encompasses more than numbers in an account—it includes the freedom to live intentionally, the resilience to navigate volatility, and the fulfillment derived from meaningful work and relationships. Measuring progress holistically ensures that wealth serves life rather than defines it.

Freedom is a key metric. Time autonomy, flexibility, and control over decisions indicate whether wealth systems are effectively supporting life. A growing bank balance without increased freedom often reflects linear income rather than systemized wealth. Tracking time and optionality ensures that resources are enabling genuine life outcomes.

Resilience is equally important. Systems should be evaluated for their capacity to withstand shocks, adapt to change, and maintain progress under stress. Diversification, anti-fragile structures, and risk management contribute to financial durability. Measuring resilience prevents illusionary security and ensures long-term sustainability.

Fulfillment reflects alignment with purpose. Wealth should create opportunities for meaningful experiences, personal growth, and impact. Metrics of satisfaction, contribution, and engagement complement financial indicators. Ignoring fulfillment risks building systems that produce wealth without enhancing life quality.

Efficiency and leverage can also be measured. How well do systems convert effort, capital, and time into recurring results? Are resources aligned with long-term objectives or dissipated in consumption? Assessing leverage and efficiency ensures that compounding potential is fully realized.

Health, relationships, and energy are additional indicators. Financial freedom is limited if physical or mental health, social connections, or personal energy are neglected. Integrating these dimensions into progress tracking creates a comprehensive view of wealth and its practical benefits.

Mindset metrics are valuable too. Patience, adaptability, ethical decision-making, and continuous learning contribute to wealth creation and sustainability. Measuring growth in these areas ensures that human capital is developing alongside financial systems.

Ultimately, wealth is multidimensional. Focusing solely on net worth risks misalignment with life goals and long-term freedom. By incorporating freedom, resilience, fulfillment, efficiency, and human capital, progress measurement becomes meaningful and actionable, guiding decisions that compound value across all dimensions.

Reflection

I once evaluated success purely by financial statements. Over time, I realized that true wealth encompassed freedom, resilience, and fulfillment. Shifting focus from numbers to holistic metrics transformed both my decisions and the outcomes of my systems, creating durable, meaningful wealth.

"Net worth is a tool, not a measure of life."

— Naval Ravikant

Chapter .38

Scaling Without Sacrificing Meaning

Growth should enhance life, not hollow it out.

Scaling systems, businesses, or assets often comes with the temptation to sacrifice values, relationships, or personal well-being. True wealth growth enhances life rather than diminishes it. By designing scalable systems that prioritize purpose, alignment, and sustainability, one can achieve expansion without compromising meaning or long-term fulfillment.

Intentional design is central. Every system should be assessed for its ability to operate at scale without demanding disproportionate personal effort or eroding core values. Processes, automation, and delegation are aligned to maintain integrity while expanding output. Growth becomes a lever for freedom and impact, not a source of stress.

Leverage amplifies scaling while preserving meaning. Using technology, other people's time, and capital strategically allows expansion without overextension. Ethical delegation and empowerment ensure that contributions multiply without compromising standards or relationships. Scale becomes sustainable and intentional.

Boundaries protect meaning. Limits on time, commitments, and risk prevent overreach and burnout. Growth is pursued thoughtfully, with systems designed to maintain balance between output and personal fulfillment. Without boundaries, scaling leads to hollow success and fragile wealth.

Monitoring feedback is critical. Metrics beyond financial returns—employee satisfaction, system efficiency, personal energy, and life alignment—ensure that scaling enhances rather than diminishes quality. Adjustments are made proactively to maintain harmony between growth and purpose.

The mindset shift is essential. Builders view scale as an opportunity to amplify impact and freedom, not as a measure of ego or status. Success is redefined as sustainable expansion that improves both systems and life. Growth without meaning is avoided by conscious intention at every step.

Sustainability compounds wealth over time. Scalable systems that operate without continuous personal input allow freedom to increase alongside output. Ethical, resilient, and efficient structures ensure that growth is self-reinforcing and durable. Expansion becomes a tool, not a trap.

Collaboration strengthens meaningful scale. Teams, partners, and stakeholders aligned with values contribute to compounding impact. Shared vision ensures that scaling benefits all parties and enhances collective purpose. Wealth becomes a byproduct of alignment, not compromise.

Ultimately, scaling without sacrificing meaning preserves both wealth and life. Growth becomes a force for freedom, impact, and fulfillment rather than stress, compromise, or hollow achievement. Systems that scale responsibly amplify the value of money, time, and human capital simultaneously.

CHAPTER .39

TURNING WEALTH INTO IMPACT

Money becomes powerful when it improves lives beyond your own.

Wealth reaches its highest potential when it extends beyond personal benefit. Turning financial resources into meaningful impact multiplies value, influence, and fulfillment. Whether through philanthropy, business innovation, or mentorship, leveraging wealth to improve lives creates compounding social, economic, and personal returns that far exceed the limits of individual gain.

Impact begins with intention. Identifying areas where resources can create tangible improvement—communities, industries, or global challenges—aligns financial power with meaningful purpose. Strategic deployment ensures that wealth generates outcomes rather than temporary gratification. Intentionality transforms money into a tool for systemic change.

Leverage amplifies impact. Capital, time, and systems can be used to mobilize others, scale solutions, and address challenges efficiently. By designing initiatives that empower people, automate processes, or replicate solutions, one dollar can create value far beyond its face amount. Multiplying influence through leverage turns personal wealth into collective growth.

Ethical principles guide long-term impact. Systems that exploit, manipulate, or harm are unsustainable and counterproductive. Wealth deployed ethically builds trust, credibility, and enduring relationships. Long-term success and societal benefit are intertwined when purpose and ethics guide decisions.

Education and mentorship extend impact exponentially. Teaching skills, providing guidance, and sharing knowledge allows others to multiply resources and ideas. These systems ensure that wealth is not a finite resource but a compounding catalyst for innovation, opportunity, and empowerment.

Feedback loops enhance effectiveness. Measuring outcomes, learning from failures, and iterating on strategies ensure that impact continues to grow. Systems that adapt and respond to results achieve sustainable change. The ability to adjust and optimize creates a self-reinforcing cycle of value creation.

Balance personal and systemic impact. While generosity and contribution are critical, sustainability requires maintaining personal and system resources. Leveraging wealth responsibly ensures that giving, investing, and scaling do not compromise long-term growth. Impact should amplify, not deplete, compounding potential.

The mindset shift is transformative. Builders see money as a vehicle for change, influence, and empowerment rather than merely comfort or status. Wealth becomes a tool for improving lives, solving problems, and leaving a legacy that endures. Purpose and profit align when impact is prioritized.

Ultimately, turning wealth into impact elevates both the individual and society. Financial systems are designed not just to generate income but to create cascading benefits. Ethical leverage, scalability, and intentionality transform personal wealth into a force for long-term, compounding improvement in the world.

Chapter .40

Building a System That Outlasts You

The highest form of wealth continues creating value after you are gone.

True wealth transcends personal lifetime; it is measured by the systems, structures, and impact that persist beyond individual existence. Building a system that outlasts you transforms wealth from a temporal resource into a lasting legacy. Assets, knowledge, and influence continue to generate value, freedom, and opportunity for future generations.

Start with durable systems. Whether financial, business, or social, the structures must be resilient, automated, and scalable. Anti-fragility, redundancy, and adaptability ensure that the system can endure shocks and changes over time. Longevity requires intentional design rather than reliance on luck or single-person effort.

Knowledge transfer is essential. Document processes, strategies, and lessons learned to ensure that successors can operate and evolve the system. Mentorship, education, and clear frameworks preserve institutional memory. Human capital, when nurtured and empowered, maintains the system's functionality long after the original builder is absent.

Ethical principles guide sustainability. Systems built on trust, integrity, and purpose are more likely to survive and grow. Exploitative, unsustainable, or opaque systems crumble when the original operator departs. Embedding values into the core ensures continuity and positive impact.

Scalable assets amplify legacy. Intellectual property, digital systems, businesses, and recurring revenue streams continue to create wealth without constant oversight. Compounding effects allow one-time effort to produce long-term returns. The focus shifts from immediate control to persistent value creation.

Succession planning secures continuity. Identifying capable individuals, establishing governance structures, and distributing authority ensures that systems remain functional and aligned with objectives. Thoughtful planning prevents disruption, preserves compounding, and maintains long-term impact.

Impact beyond wealth is paramount. Systems that outlast their creator extend influence, education, and opportunity to others. Social contributions, philanthropic initiatives, and community-oriented projects magnify the effect of wealth beyond financial returns. Legacy becomes multidimensional.

Automation and feedback loops reinforce sustainability. Systems that self-correct, adapt, and optimize ensure durability. Processes, monitoring, and measurable outcomes allow the system to evolve autonomously. Compounding continues, not just financially but in influence, knowledge, and social impact.

Ultimately, building a system that outlasts you represents the pinnacle of wealth thinking. It transcends individual effort, creating freedom, optionality, and influence for generations. True wealth is immortalized in systems, knowledge, and impact that compound far beyond a single lifetime.

Reflection

I once focused on building wealth only for myself, without considering longevity or legacy. Shifting to creating systems that endure transformed my approach. The knowledge, processes, and scalable structures I designed now continue to generate value, influence, and opportunity, proving that lasting systems are the ultimate form of wealth.

"Legacy is wealth that compounds beyond your lifetime."
— Unknown

Epilogue

As we close this book, remember that wealth is not found in a salary, a title, or even a bank balance. It is a living, breathing system that compounds when designed intentionally. Every principle, mindset shift, and system you build is a brick in the foundation of your long-term freedom and impact.

The journey will never be "complete"—systems evolve, challenges arise, and opportunities expand. The real power lies in understanding that you are the architect of your own wealth. You are no longer a passive participant in a broken salary system; you are the designer of a framework that multiplies your effort, preserves your time, and creates lasting impact.

Your next step is to act. Build, iterate, and refine. Share what you learn. Protect your downside, amplify your upside, and focus relentlessly on freedom, not just income. When you design your life as a system, wealth is no longer a goal—it becomes the natural outcome of deliberate, purposeful action.

About the Author

Laura Lee is a writer, entrepreneur, and systems thinker dedicated to bridging creativity, innovation, and human potential. She has spent her career designing frameworks that empower individuals and brands to create clarity, purpose, and impact in both life and work.

As the founder of a successful digital design agency, Laura has helped countless people and organizations translate vision into actionable systems that scale. Her work reflects her belief that wealth is not a number but a structure—one that compounds freedom, influence, and opportunity when thoughtfully built.

Through her books, digital platforms, and creative consulting, Laura inspires others to see beyond linear thinking, embrace intentional systems, and design lives of autonomy, meaning, and impact. She believes that money, time, and creativity are tools—not goals—and that true success lies in building frameworks that outlast us while enhancing the lives of others.

This book is an extension of that mission: a guide to building systems that generate freedom, resilience, and lasting impact in a world that often values appearances over substance.